ON THE WATER

ON THE WATER

The Romance and Lore
of America's Small Boats

Text and illustrations by Douglas Alvord

A division of
Yankee Publishing Incorporated
Dublin, New Hampshire

Designed by Eugenie Seidenberg
Yankee Publishing Incorporated
Dublin, New Hampshire
First Edition
Copyright 1988 by Douglas Alvord
Printed in the United States of America.

Drawing on page 122 based on Winslow Homer's
Breezing Up.
Drawings on pages 58, 59, 64, 69, and 70 courtesy of the
Maine Maritime Museum, Bath, Maine.

On the Water text was typeset in Garamond Condensed
by Yankee Graphics, Dublin, New Hampshire, and
printed on cream white Stora Matte by The Meriden-
Stinehour Press, Lunenburg, Vermont; the dust jacket and
four-color artwork were printed by New England Book
Components, Hingham, Massachusetts. The book was
bound at The Book Press, Inc., Brattleboro, Vermont.

Alvord, Douglas.
   On the water: the romance and lore of America's small
boats / text and illustrations by Douglas Alvord. — 1st ed.
        p.   cm.
   Bibliography: p.
   Includes index.
   ISBN 0-89909-157-1 : $24.95
   1. Boats and boating — United States. 2. Navigation —
United States. 3. United States — History, Naval.   I.
Title.
VK23.A745 1988
623.8'202'0974—dc 19   87-31654
                                           CIP

DEDICATION

To the many builders and designers over
the course of American maritime history who,
by their skills, instinct for design, and sound
understanding of the ways of the water, have left
us a legacy of fine small watercraft. Because of
their efforts, we are able to understand the
development of our maritime heritage and to
enjoy the pleasures of this proud tradition.

ACKNOWLEDGMENTS

This book has been an ongoing project for a number of years and was made possible by the kind encouragement of numerous friends in the boating industry; by the open cooperation of many maritime museums and their staffs; and most especially by the generous help of the builders themselves, who gave me firsthand accounts of the practices and finer points of small-boat building and shared their personal recollections of a time gone by. I wish to thank all of these people for their assistance and support; I am pleased that they share a common interest in the documentation of both the cultural and social history of small boats.

My personal thanks to Eugenie Seidenberg for her handsome layout and design, and to Sandy Taylor for her patience and willingness to shape my manuscript into decent prose, while she learned at the same time a "foreign" language — the mariner's tongue.

I am also grateful to my literary agent, Jacques de Spoelberch, for his personal encouragement of my work and his professional commitment to good publishing.

CONTENTS

FOREWORD

Over the years Doug Alvord has been a good friend to the Maine Maritime Museum, and his work is seen throughout the organization in exhibits, catalogs, and the other ephemera the museum publishes. His particular facility is rendering the complex into terms that are easily understood by those of us with the interest, but not the inclination, to study a subject in minutia. He possesses this gift in both writing and drawing. Thus, *On the Water* is a natural subject for Doug, given his proclivity toward wanting to be there himself.

I first met Doug on a boat some years ago. We were making a short weekend passage out of Newport, Rhode Island, and fell into talking about our work, which has similarities. He told me at that time that he was leaving Nantucket, which was losing its charm to upscale development, and moving to Maine to

concentrate more on marine-related fine art.

Just as winter began to settle in on the coast, Doug came to my office and asked how he could help out at the museum. It wasn't long before he and Irma, his wife, were thoroughly enmeshed in a variety of activities, from technical drawing and speaking to our membership to doing research along the coast.

Chapter Four in this book was drawn largely from a winter that Doug and I spent traveling from Bath to Jonesport and Beals Island to do research on the lobster boat, a unique Maine workboat. The work, in part sponsored by the National Endowment for the Arts, and the material gathered aided immeasurably in the development of a major exhibit and catalog on lobstering done by the museum in 1985. Of course, to do this type of research properly, we had to pick what had to be one of the coldest winters along the coast. My memories are of Doug sketching with blue fingers, trying to capture a detail on how a sternpost was fitted or a stem pieced together. Often it wasn't much better inside the shops of the builders, who liked to keep the heat low (if there was any at all) because, as they explained, it kept them from getting "logy." All in all it was a tough assignment, but one that was necessary to our understanding not only of the boats, but also of the culture in which they developed. We made a lot of friends that winter and heard a variety of opinions on what it is that makes a boat go on the water.

I imagine this book developed out of that winter and many others like it when Doug has had the time to give shape to his experiences afloat and ashore "talking boats," which is the favorite pastime here along the coast. His other experiences as a designer and builder of watercraft also have contributed to this project. The writing here is enthusiastic yet approachable, unlike much of what has been produced by others in the past.

Few people today have a sense of the diversity of our traditional small craft heritage,

and this book fills a niche in our cultural history. It explains in a readable format why boats have been and continue to be important to us. In recent years there has been a renewed interest in traditional watercraft, fueled by increasing leisure time, new publications, and, I'm happy to say, maritime museums that have taken the time to preserve and document small boats.

More than once, it has been asked what good is a museum where everything is locked up and can't be used for fear of damage or, in the case of historic watercraft, of sinking? It takes people like Doug, and some of the builders mentioned in this text, to push the boats and the interest out the museum doors and into the public domain. I call them enablers because they work with us to reach a wider audience and have shown us how we might be more effective in letting people know about good boats.

People like them were responsible for the Maine Maritime Museum's founding a school of boatbuilding. The Apprenticeshop, as it is called, has trained more than one hundred fifty young people who have learned by doing: building traditional wooden boats. Many of the tenets we stress to students come through quite clearly in *On the Water.*

There is a rewarding sense of individuality and freedom that comes through hands-on activities, whether building or using a small boat. Because the activity is on a personal level, it creates a deep sense of achievement, something that is important in our world of high technology and mass production. We all need time to contemplate and assess the directions our lives are taking, and for an increasing number of people, that time has been found while drifting or purposefully heading out in a small boat. It is hoped that this book will draw even more people into this enriching pastime.

John Swain Carter
Director
Maine Maritime Museum
Bath, Maine

INTRODUCTION

The first time a human floated downstream on a log, he found it not only a fast way to travel but an enjoyable one, too. When he hollowed out the log, he could carry goods and keep a little drier, and when he later found a way to build his craft from ribs and some sort of covering, it was faster and lighter. Eventually, he added poles to push it; still later oars for rowing; and at some point when he held up a cloth in the way of the breeze . . . sail was born.

We have come a long way, through the grand age of great sailing ships to huge tankers that are longer than some small ponds. But most of our contemporary vessels are somewhat impersonal and deny us close contact or a sense of being on the water. This is not so with small craft, which are readily accessible and provide essentially the same experience they have for centuries.

Watercraft have always developed out of need, and most boats have worked for a living, whether as transport, trader, fishing craft, or hunting boat. There are fewer working small watercraft today, and many traditional types have been adapted for personal recreational use. There was a demand for small boats after World War II, but unfortunately, in the scramble to meet that demand, much of the tradition was lost. Mass-produced aluminum and fiberglass boats at first bore little resemblance to their forebears, and compromised some of their predecessors' age-proven seaworthiness as well.

Happily, a renaissance is taking place in the building, use, and appreciation of small boats. New techniques are once again making wood a viable building material, and fine publications such as *WoodenBoat, Small Boat Journal,* and *Messing About In Boats* are spreading the word.

The fact that something of good design, useful purpose, and personal pleasure can survive in our high-tech society is a tribute to the traditional wooden boat. To be sure, they had to adapt, but with the vision of those who have continued to preserve and promote small boats, and the many who enjoy their special qualities, we are able to perpetuate the tradition.

Necessity has been the commissioner of boat design, and specific local conditions and available materials the developer. Consequently, the seaworthy Maine lobster boat has spawned many small powerboats; the Chesapeake skipjack (still used today for oystering) has inspired more than one fast pleasure boat; and both the eighteenth-century peapod and the canoe have influenced contemporary rowing boats. Most of these boats were developed hundreds of miles from each other, and the skills and designs were passed on largely by word of mouth, yet there is a common theme that seems to have influenced boat design for centuries: Common sense and experience are the best teachers. Workboats might be expected to be purely utilitarian, and their construction for the most part is straightforward and practical. But out of that simplicity often comes a sweet sense of beauty. To my mind, even though I am familiar with and delighted by a great variety of boats, nothing seems to typify this combination of beauty and purposefulness more than a skipjack, old and none too tidy, gliding across the bay with its huge mainsail and jib set on a raking mast, its graceful sheer dipping and rising over clear summer waters under a breezy blue sky.

There are hundreds of boats indigenous to our country — each with its own history, romance, and unique qualities — but this would have been a heavy volume indeed had I tried to catalog, document, or sketch them all. Certain types, such as skin boats, are not included here because I chose those craft that were in common usage in a few geographical areas. The examples I do discuss are largely East Coast vessels because most American watercraft started here.

On the Water is meant to be an introduction to selected small boats — both working and pleasure craft. You will meet some of the people who have contributed to the heritage, customs, and pleasures of their boats.

You will see how small boats are constructed, have developed, and are used and preserved. In addition to giving you an overview, I hope the book also inspires you to do further reading and to visit the many museums and boat shops where these watercraft can be seen. A list of sources is included in the back of the book.

On the Water is not only about small boats, it is also about spirit . . . freedom . . . individuality. Riding in even the simplest plywood skiff can be an enriching experience, for in this age when many of our work efforts and even pastimes are unfulfilling, there is something extremely satisfying about the intimate pleasure of being on the water.

CHAPTER ONE

Boat
Basics

Small boats are a product of need — a specific type for a specific purpose — and are made to operate in local, not global, waters. To this extent, there are boats that have existed virtually unchanged for more than two thousand years.

Although the history of large sailing ships is well documented, that of small craft is not. Perhaps it is because the latter have been largely workboats and therefore not featured in historic and romantic literature. In 1930 Howard Chapelle, a boat designer, began a serious study of our native coastal working craft, and in 1951 he published what has become a classic: *American Small Sailing Craft*. This detailed document is a welcome source for understanding the development of our maritime heritage. It is primarily a technical work in which Mr. Chapelle has painstakingly recorded the designs of a wide variety of boats, many of which no longer exist. Equally important, however, is the cultural and social history surrounding the use and development of small boats — a rich part of the history of our country.

When the earliest settlers arrived in the New World, fishing quickly became a necessary occupation; farming entailed the clearing and development of land, and the hungry population simply could not idly wait while this was being done. As early as 1622, British fishermen had established a salt-cod drying station on Damariscove Island, off the midcoast area of Maine. The Damariscove fishermen used shallops and small sloops they had brought with them from England, but they soon realized they needed boats more suitable for the local waters and more simply built than the complicated craft they had on hand. Consequently, our American maritime heritage began to evolve.

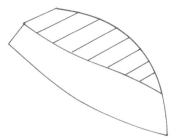

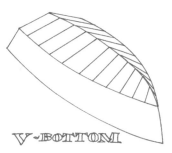

Perhaps the best way to understand small boats is to look at just what a boat has to do: It must keep the water out, carry a load, and move through the water with efficiency and safety. The dugout made sense initially, and in certain limited applications it is still being used today. But because it is heavy and narrow, it is not an efficient vessel. Building techniques became more sophisticated as boats began to be constructed out of more than one piece of wood. The pieces had to be joined together so as not to leak, and in order to make a shell-like structure that would be lighter, the pieces had to be braced in some fashion to resist the strong pressure water exerts on the underwater portion of the boat. Thus, the dugout eventually gave way to planked boats assembled over some sort of frame or rib structure — a method that remained predominant until the present age of plastics.

Plank-on-frame construction is used in the three basic hull configurations. The simplest is a sort of flat-bottomed box, with one end pointed so as to move the boat more easily through the water. A refinement of this is to have the bottom deeper in the middle than at the ends; the sides

of such a boat might be square to the bottom or flared out a little for better seaworthiness when the boat heels, or tips.

Almost everyone has seen or been in a rowboat or skiff. A skiff is perfectly suitable for certain needs — such as carrying a heavy load in a relatively small space. It is easily planked and requires little bending of the wood. Since all wood swells naturally when immersed in water, if the planks are nailed tightly together, the well-built boat will not leak after its initial launching. Early on, whenever people needed quick transportation on a river, they built boats right on the banks and often abandoned them after reaching their destination. But since such boats were largely rowed, or sailed with a very inefficient sail downwind, they did not move very easily.

One way to improve on this was to make the bottom a shallow V, thus raising the lower edge (chine) of the side to displace less water. In the V-bottomed boat, the construction is more sophisticated, and the frames play an important role in shaping the boat. With a more complex shape, the planks must be steamed or soaked in hot water to assume their shape, and due to greater stresses caused by the sprung wood, the boat must have a skeleton that will be strong enough to hold and maintain this shape. Straight nails, such as the square-cut iron ones used in house building, do not hold well and tend to rust. Because screws were not available to early American boatbuilders, trunnels (tree nails) were often used, the heads of which could be forced apart with a spline. As the nails swelled, they prevented the planks from working loose.

Without power tools and modern-day fastenings and glues, these early small craft had to be kept simple. For frames to be strong, they could not consist of too many pieces; thus the builder looked for "natural" frames, such as crooks in the roots or larger branches of trees, which could be sawn to fit the curved shape of the boat.

The V-bottomed boat is still a popular configuration that has proved very stable, fast, and seaworthy — especially in workboats such as the Chesapeake Bay skipjack, a design almost unchanged for a hundred years. It entails a comparatively inexpensive method of building; for the most part, it requires planks to be bent only in one direction at a time, which makes it especially suitable for plywood construction.

A V-bottomed boat is ideal for carrying heavy loads, but when a light rowing boat is desired, such as a Whitehall, a round-bottomed boat is faster and more maneuverable. Since Egyptian times, people have found ways to construct round-bottomed boats from straight wood. Making the frames was not that difficult, either by steaming ribs in a curve, as the Indians did for canoes, or by sawing frames from natural crooks. But the planking had to be made to fit a shape it does not naturally take. To see how this is accomplished, look at a wooden barrel. The staves are bent to fit the shape and cut so they taper somewhat at the ends. Thus, when they come together, there is a roundness to the shape in two directions at once.

By the advent of the schooner, round-bottomed boatbuilding in this country had produced some very fast and extremely handsome watercraft. But the evolution of all three forms — flat-bottomed, V-bottomed, and round-bottomed — makes up small craft history, and the variations provide us with a rich maritime heritage.

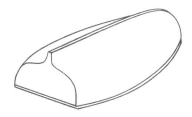

ROUND-BOTTOM

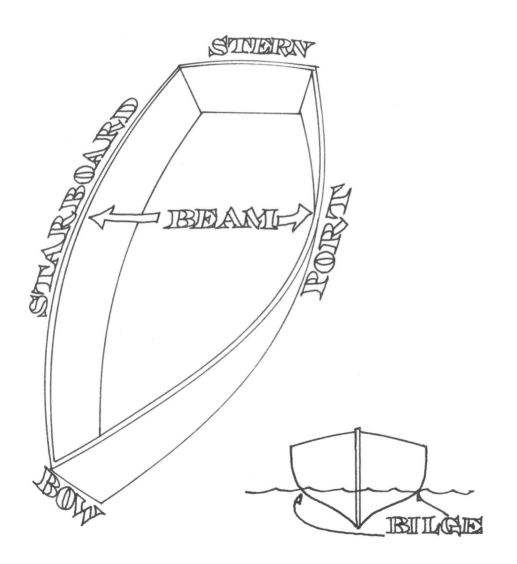

While not intended as a course in boatbuilding, the following general information should help the uninitiated better understand the building process and how it relates to the development of the early water trades. This section is arranged not in alphabetical order, but by terms that belong together, as if you were walking around the boat, having a discussion about it.

Boat Orientation

BOW – the extreme front end of any boat.

STERN – the extreme back end; may be square, pointed, or rounded.

PORT – the left side of a boat, facing forward.

STARBOARD – the right side, facing forward.

BEAM – the widest part of a boat across its center.

BILGE – both the lowest part of the boat inside and the point at which the bottom meets the sides. The sharper the angle at this point, the stiffer and more stable the boat.

FREEBOARD – the height of the hull above the water.

WATERLINE – the points where the water's surface touches the boat. Waterline length is the distance at the waterline from the point farthest forward to the point farthest aft.

DRAFT – the depth and volume of a boat below the waterline.

HULL – the body of the boat, which gives it its shape (excluding masts, yards, sails, and rigging).

Structure and Construction

SHEER – the top edge of the boat's sides, from stem to stern. Sometimes referred to as the gunwale.

SHEER CLAMP OR INWALE – the piece of wood that ties together the frame on the inside and strengthens the sheer.

CENTERBOARD – a retractable fin that when down keeps a boat sailing on course and when up allows a boat to venture into shallow water.

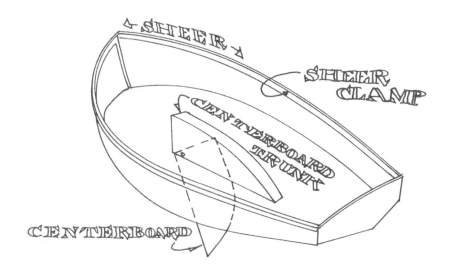

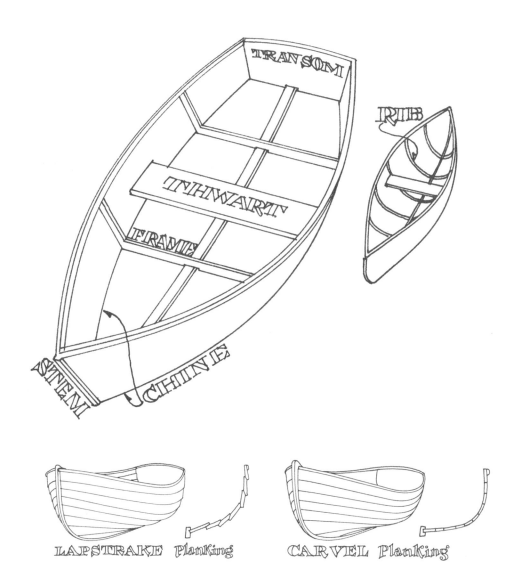

LAPSTRAKE Planking   CARVEL Planking

FRAME – the structural member centered on the keel, or backbone, that forms the shape of the boat and holds the planking. It can be either sawn or bent.

RIB – similar to a frame but generally inserted after the hull is formed; tends to be of a slender dimension, bent into place.

STEM – a vertical timber at the bow to which the sides and keel are fastened.

TRANSOM – the planking across the stern, except in double-ended boats, which have an aft stem instead.

LAPSTRAKE – a type of planking where the edges of the boards overlap slightly.

CARVEL – a type of planking where the edges of the boards fit flush to each other.

CHINE – in flat or V-bottomed boats, the point where the sides meet the bottom.

THWART – a plank across the boat used as a seat.

GARBOARD – the plank next to the keel, and often the one most difficult to form, as it tends to be nearly horizontal amidships and twists to almost vertical at the stem.

RUDDER – a bladelike device mounted aft to turn the boat.

TILLER – a lever arm attached to the rudder by which the boat is steered.

COAMING – a splashboard on the deck at the edge of the cockpit.

KNEE – an L-shaped piece sometimes cut from the natural curve in a tree, added to parts of the boat that take a greater strain, such as where the hull meets the deck.

SKEG – on boats that do not have a full or external keel, a small "fin" that is added aft to help the boat row or track straight.

KEEL – the spine or backbone of a boat; also, in a sailing craft, the weighted, vertical part below the bottom to give a boat stability and offset the side pressure of the wind on the sails.

BALLAST – usually lead in the keel, or in some cases rocks or lead ingots placed low inside a boat, to aid stability in rough seas.

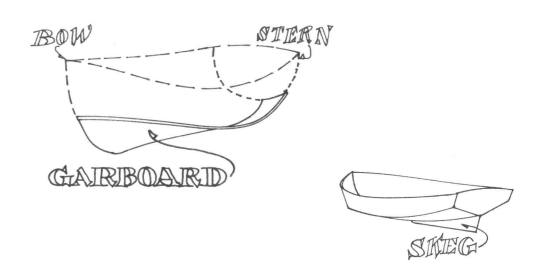

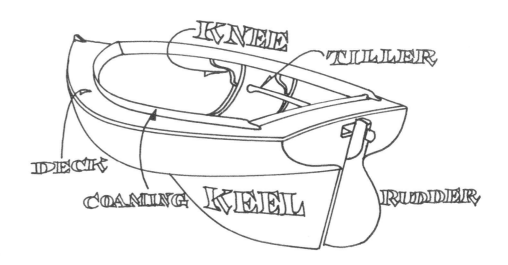

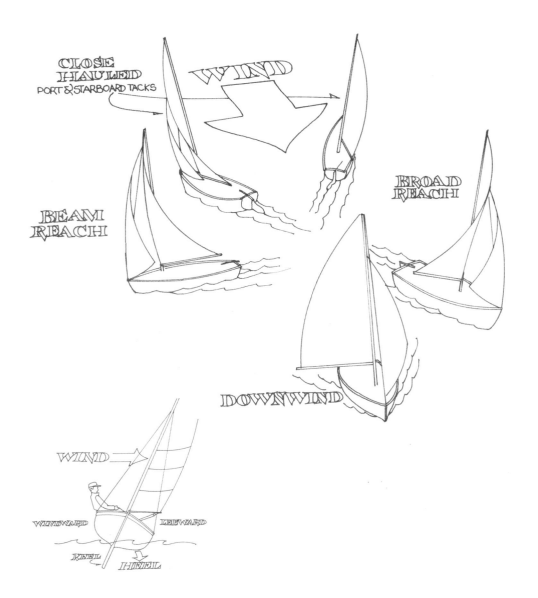

Movement

HULL SPEED — since boats must displace their own weight in water when moving under oar or sail, they can rarely exceed the designed hull speed: a formula generally accepted as the square root of the waterline length times $1\frac{4}{10}$. (Thus, a 16-footer would move at about $5\frac{1}{2}$ knots.) The exception would be when under power, though there are limitations to this as well, since an overpowered boat would tend to "skip" and lose its efficiency.

HEEL — under sail a boat will heel, or tip to one side. The amount of heel is determined by the stiffness of the bilge shape, the ballast, and/or the depth of keel.

WINDWARD AND LEEWARD — toward the wind and away from the wind. The windward side is the side of the boat that the wind blows onto; the leeward side is the other side.

GO TO WINDWARD — originally all a boat could do under sail was go downwind, but as the art of sailing developed, a combination of boat design and type of rig made it possible for a vessel to move against the wind at an angle, with the leeway counteracted by the keel or centerboard.

BEAM REACH – the point of sail when the wind is bearing directly on the side of the boat.

BROAD REACH – the point of sail when the wind is bearing from the rear quarter of the boat.

TACK – to bring the boat from one windward course to the other.

STABILITY – a boat's ability to stay upright and not heel or tip. Boats that are wide or that have deep, heavy keels are more stable than narrow boats and boats without keels.

Small Craft Rigs

MAST – the vertical pole, tapered toward the top, that holds the sail; usually cut from an appropriately sized tree, though sometimes made up of pieces in either square or round sections.

BOOM – the horizontal spar fixed along the

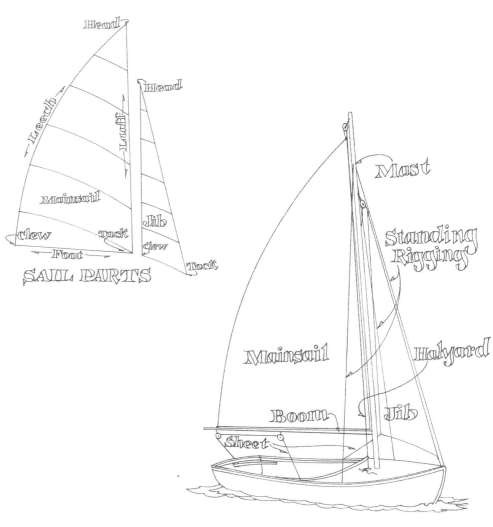

SAIL PARTS

MARCONI RIG

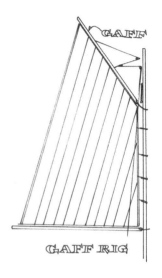

GAFF

GAFF RIG

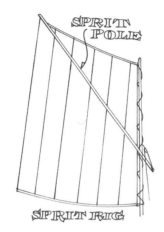

SPRIT POLE

SPRIT RIG

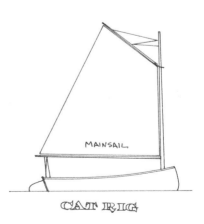

MAINSAIL

CAT RIG

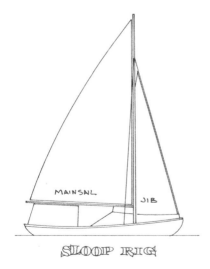

MAINSAIL

JIB

SLOOP RIG

bottom of the sail to help keep its shape and control its movement.

GAFF — a spar used at the top of a four-sided sail, which slides on the mast.

SHEET — ropes that are used in conjunction with blocks to control the sails; also known as the running rigging.

STANDING RIGGING — shrouds or ropes fastened to the mast and secured to the boat to keep the mast standing under pressure of the sails.

HALYARD — a rope used to raise or lower a sail.

MAINSAIL — in all cases, the main or principal sail.

MIZZEN — generally a smaller sail, set aft of the mainsail.

JIB — one or more smaller, triangular sails set forward to help the boat move to windward.

BATTEN — a short stiffener inserted in a pocket in the leech to help hold the curved shape of the sail.

MARCONI RIG – a mainsail with three sides: the foot, which is the bottom; the luff, which runs up the mast; and the leech, which is the after edge.

GAFF RIG – a mainsail with four sides, a boom at the bottom, and a gaff boom at the top edge.

SPRIT RIG – a four-sided mainsail with a sprit pole.

CAT RIG – any rig without a jib.

SLOOP RIG – a mainsail on a single mast set with only one jib.

CUTTER RIG – a rig that is set with one mainsail and two or more jibs.

KETCH RIG – two masts, with the main taller than the mizzen. The mizzen is set forward of the tiller; usually set with one or more jibs.

YAWL RIG – tall mainsail with small mizzen set aft of the tiller; usually set with a jib.

SCHOONER RIG – two masts with the foremast shorter than the aftermast; usually set with one or more jibs.

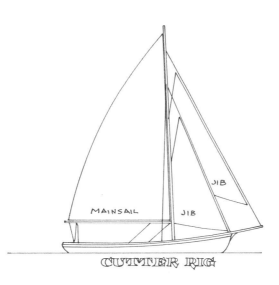

CUTTER RIG

KETCH RIG

YAWL RIG

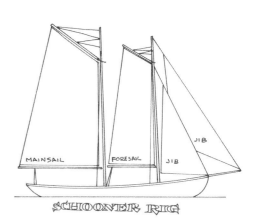

SCHOONER RIG

CHAPTER TWO

THE NATIVE AMERICAN BOAT

Spring has come to the land of the northern Indians. From Maine to Vancouver Island, the white paper birch is in prime condition for canoe building. (By summer the heat will have rendered it too brittle.) Each tribe is gathering to decide on how many canoes it will need for the year ahead. With this done, the master builder dispatches two braves to the woods to find the trees tall enough to have an 18-foot span of bark free of branches and mature enough to make a whole skin. One young man climbs a tree and makes a clean cut all around it, then a single slit as he descends to the bottom, carefully peeling back the bark to loosen it as he goes. When the braves return, they have several perfect skins, ready to become canoes. In the meantime, the older men gather white cedar, which will become interior sheathing, ribs, and gunwales, and the women scrape gum from the spruce trees, placing it in birch-bark cones to be boiled for the pitch needed to seal the joints and holes.

The tools used are bone, flint, and beaver teeth. The master builder has a memory stick — a piece of birch upon which he has cut notches to keep track of the essential dimensions of the design — but that is all. From this he arranges short stakes in the ground between which the water-softened bark is laid. Using the memory stick for dimensions, he cuts two long cedar rails, which are tied together and then spread apart to form the shape of the canoe.

The next morning the women split long spruce roots in half, using their teeth to hold one end. Young boys start two large fires while the builder shows others how to split and smooth the cedar for the ribs — each about 5 feet long and 2 inches wide. One of the fires is in a hollow

Although each job was assigned and supervised by the master builder, canoe building was usually a community effort as well as a social event.

in the earth. The fire is raked out and the hole filled with water, the ribs are put in, and the water is kept boiling with stones from the other fire. When the ribs are soft enough, the old master bends them into a U and ties the whole lot together to keep their shape. Nested inside each other, they take the form of a canoe, which narrows toward the ends.

On the next day, if the weather is warm (which helps keep the bark supple), the women gather around the U-shaped bark, and using spruce roots, they sew the general shape together, using extra pieces of bark at each end where the bow and stern rise higher. With six or eight women to a boat, this allows time for socializing and for the older women to repeat tribal stories and legends to the young girls.

The old master determines the exact shape the canoe ends will have (an indicator of which region the canoe comes from), and after he cuts this shape and carefully bends stem and stern pieces, the women bind these in. Laced from end to end, very thin pieces of cedar are used to form the interior sheathing, because bark alone is not strong enough. The master fits the permanent ribs, hammering them gently into place so that

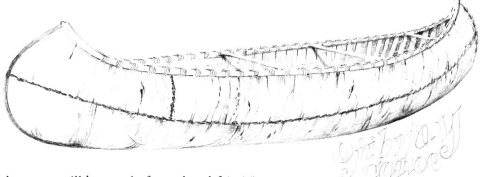

the canoe will be evenly formed and fair. Then the women seal every seam and lace hole with the spruce pitch, carefully tucking a little packet of it up under the bow for repairs. Finally, with great ceremony, the master takes the canoe to the water, proving his agility by stepping into it just as it leaves the edge of the bank. If it is suitable, he signals the beginning of another.

This was a typical operation, but the exact method of making a birch-bark canoe and its form varied from tribe to tribe. The Micmac Indians, for instance, built canoes with sides that were high in the middle; the Ojibway canoes resembled those most familiar to us.

The history of the canoe is global and far too complex for the scope of this book. A beautifully executed study, published in 1983 by International Marine Publishing of Camden,

The method used for constructing a birch-bark canoe varied among the Indian tribes, and it is the shape of the ends of the craft, determined by the master builder, that indicates the region in which the canoe was built.

*High-bowed Alaskan
dugout canoe.*

*Primitive single-log
dugout canoe.*

*Facing page: Florida swamp
canoe with cut-away bow and
flaring gunwales.*

Maine, is titled *The Canoe: A History of the Craft
from Panama to the Arctic* by Kenneth Roberts
and Philip Shackleton. In the book are examples
of canoes that are remarkably similar to each
other but have no known geographic
connection. For example, it is unlikely that the
Indians of New England would have traveled to
the Pacific Northwest, but canoes from both
regions closely resemble each other, both in basic
design and construction.

In its most basic form, a boat is simply the
most logical way of getting on the water; its
development stems from the need to adapt a
vessel to a specific task, plus the natural human
instinct to "tinker." We began with logs, then
rafts, then dugouts. A prehistoric pictograph,

found on a rock face in Ontario, shows a
number of people in what is clearly some sort of
canoelike vessel, with raised bow and stern and
two paddlers. Most likely it is a dugout. Using
scraper and hand axes, early people in all parts
of the world hollowed out logs to make a more
comfortable, seaworthy, and load-carrying craft.

Dugout canoes (as well as bark canoes in
the north) were in full use in America at the
time of the early settlers and were among the
first boats the settlers began to adopt for their
own uses. As a species, the dugout reached a
high level of sophistication — from the very large
high-bowed Alaskan boats with carved and
painted figureheads to the more modest but
clever Florida swamp canoe that had a sharply
cut-away bow and sharp flaring gunwale
forward to slice through the thick and dangerous
saw grass.

In the seventeenth century, as the early
settlers pushed inland, they became acquainted
with the bark canoe. The boats they had
brought with them were of little use inland,
being heavily planked and not easily dragged
around obstacles or across long portages when a
lake or river abruptly ended. Indians with whom

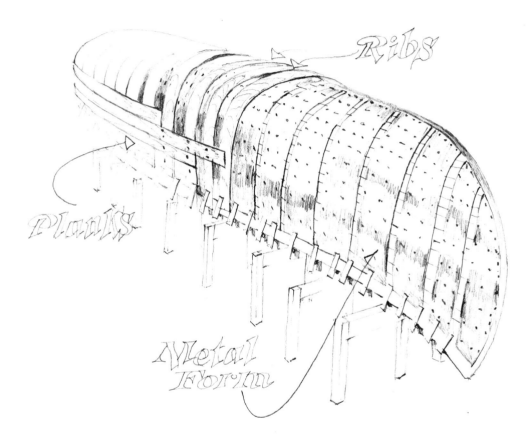

Ribs

Planks

Metal Form

Mass production of the canoe was made possible by using the master mold, a form over which the boat is fashioned.

they traded would often act as guides, easily transporting the settlers and their gear in their more suitable light canoes.

The early wilderness settler had to be self-reliant and inventive; he could not go to a

boatbuilder a hundred miles out in the bush. Most did use the Indian canoes and dugouts, but some tried to adapt the European skin boat to their needs. An early surveyor named Verplanck Colvin, chief supervisor of the Adirondack Topographical Survey, devised for himself a canvas boat that he could carry in a sack. He would fabricate the frame from willow saplings when needed and then use the framework for firewood when he got to where he was going.

Mapmaker David Thompson traveled over the Rockies to the Columbia River in 1811. In need of a canoe, he decided to build one, but he could not find any suitable bark. Instead he used thin cedar planks sewn together with spruce roots in the Indian manner.

Early settlers had sail-making canvas and soon discovered that this was excellent for sealing seams and more vulnerable parts of a canoe, such as the bow and stern. Eventually, the inevitable followed: making whole skins of the material. At the same time, several "tin" (actually Russian iron) canoes appeared, forerunners of the contemporary aluminum boats and built for the same reason — durability.

However, they were not especially appealing, as they were heavy and noisy.

By 1850 the canoe was rarely used for commerce but had become the vehicle of choice for sportsmen, many of whom had used bark canoes for years. The supply of Indian-built canoes was dwindling, however, and this marked the beginning of the manufactured boat. The Peterborough Canoe Company of Peterborough, Ontario, is generally credited with having started, or at least led the development of, this new industry.

The thousands of canoes manufactured over the past hundred years have become an indigenous part of American culture. While the Indian master builder relied on his eye to form the shape, the modern canoe builder's prize tool is the master mold. The mold is carefully built, reflecting the shape that suits the taste of its designer, and then it is sheathed with bands of metal where the ribs will fall. This is done so that when the copper tacks are driven through the planking and ribs, the points will automatically bend over, "clinching" themselves.

The ribs are flat, thin strips of cedar,

tapered at the ends and bent over the mold, then clamped in place until the planking is finished. The canvas is stretched over the canoe, pulled tight at the ends with clamps, and extended beyond the bow and stern. The edges are fastened and the ends later covered with brass half-round strips. No glue is used on the canvas, only paint to make it watertight, for it could never be replaced if it were adhered to the wood. Finally, the gunwales are installed and the seats, usually caned, added. That's all there is to a canoe – a deceptively simple boat in substance.

Fine canoe building, though, is an art, preserved and carried on by numerous small shops, each with its own special variations and finesse. This applies also to the canoe's "engine" – the paddle. The handmade paddle can be a thing of beauty, and many canoeists prefer to make their own, tailoring the shape and heft to their own style of use. But to supply the market, a means had to be found to mass-produce them. At Orono, Maine, the Shaw and Tenney Oar and Paddle Company has been in business for more than one hundred twenty-five years. Paul Regan, its current owner, still uses the shop's

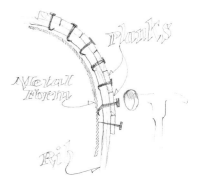

Clinch-nailing the planks of a canoe.

*Finishing a paddle on a sanding
machine at the Shaw and Tenney
shop. The objective is to make the
edges as thin as possible so the
paddle is light, while still
leaving enough of the wood to
insure strength.*

original machinery. The blanks for paddles are
cut from spruce on a bandsaw, then secured
in a lathe to turn the handles. The blades
are finished on large sanding drums with
successively finer grit before receiving a coat of
varnish. In this case, the paddles are dipped in a
long, slender varnish tank to save the time
necessary to apply the finish by hand. The
process is a careful blend of machine technology
and handcraftsmanship, and the price is still
competitive in today's market for quality
paddles.

In 1880 the American Canoe Association
was formed at Lake George, New York, for the
purpose of furthering interest in the canoe as a
cruising vessel; racing regattas — and, of course,
fancier and faster canoes — followed almost
immediately. Clubs sprang up everywhere, and
all manner of expeditions and modifications
took place. One canoe was even steam powered.
Canoe mania had struck.

At this time, the most renowned canoeist
in the country was Nathaniel Bishop. In 1874
he made a voyage from Troy, New York, to
Florida in a canoe made of paper. This intrepid
little vessel was built of many layers of what we

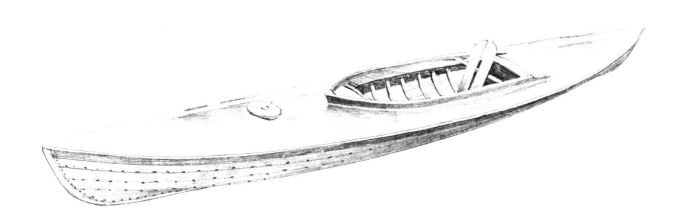

This 16-foot Rob Roy, built in 1930, was designed by L. Francis Herreshoff, who used it for many years for camp-cruising.

would today call industrial-strength paper toweling – glued, painted, and applied to a light framework. Bishop and the father of the Boy Scouts, Lord Robert Baden-Powell, founded the New York Canoe Club, which held the most sophisticated racing events of the late nineteenth century.

Some fancy canoe making got its start on the other side of the Atlantic. John MacGregor, a Scot living in London, was a proponent of what was called "muscular Christianity" – an evangelizing philosophy that sought converts through the example of sportsmanship, physical training, and athletic competition. He had traveled and canoed in this country and had

become enamored of the various canoe types. When he returned to England, he designed and built the *Rob Roy,* which was a decked, clinker-built, double-ended boat of roughly canoe proportions. It was designed to sail steadily, to paddle easily, to float lightly, and to bear rough usage. This design influenced many American canoe designers, among them Henry Rushton and W.P. Stephens, two of the leading small craft designers of the late nineteenth century.

There is a sixteenth-century engraving of "aye savauge standing inne aye canow withe sacking helde to catch breezes," indicating that the notion of sailing a canoe was not new, though doing so in such a tender and light craft

The Argonaut, *a Henry Rushton sailing canoe, was considered by many to be the ultimate cruising canoe, ideal for exploring America's wilderness areas.*

was a tricky proposition. Undaunted by this fact, those with racing blood met the challenge, and both Rushton and Stephens produced some very fast ketch-rigged vessels that windsurfers of today would envy. These boats had outrigger planks to allow the helmsman to hike out to windward (performing a fancy balancing act while coming about), to manage both sails and the rudder, and to shift the plank from one side to the other.

Almost any canoe can be rigged for more sedate sailing with a smaller sail, leeboards for stability, and a paddle for steering. Thus, touring canoeists can take advantage of favorable breezes to extend their cruising area.

*   *   *

Interest in canoes began to decline during the early part of this century, partly due to the post-World War I popularity of the outboard motor, and consequently, the major canoe manufacturers began to go out of business. Handmade wooden canoes were rarely produced, except on custom order or to supply the guide trade, and these were made by small

one- and two-man shops. In 1920, on Grand
Lake Stream in the home waters of the
Passamaquoddy tribe of Maine, boats that were
half canoe and half outboard skiff began to
appear. The area is famous for hunting and
fishing, and the Passamaquoddy had a good
trade taking sportsmen downstream in their
rigged guide canoes. A little broader than other
canoes, with a square transom, these boats,
eventually known as Grandlakers, handled well
under power, yet were still capable of being
paddled — something fishermen appreciated.

Most of the builders of the Grandlaker are
gone now, but one shop is still active. Grand
Lake Stream is a fishing town: no tennis resorts,
McDonald's, or Cadillac dealers. Salmon and
trout are king, and Kenny Wheaton, one of two
men still building the Grandlaker, is a local
legend. He started in 1946, and his boats today
are the same as when he began, except now they
are covered with fiberglass instead of canvas — a
sensible choice since recanvasing is a tough job
and no one seems to have time to do it anymore.

A company that has remained in business
as a full-time manufacturer since 1890 is the
Old Town Canoe Company on Maine's

*Kenny Wheaton with one of his
Grandlakers. Similar in
construction to a canoe, this
wider, square-stern boat is both
light and strong.*

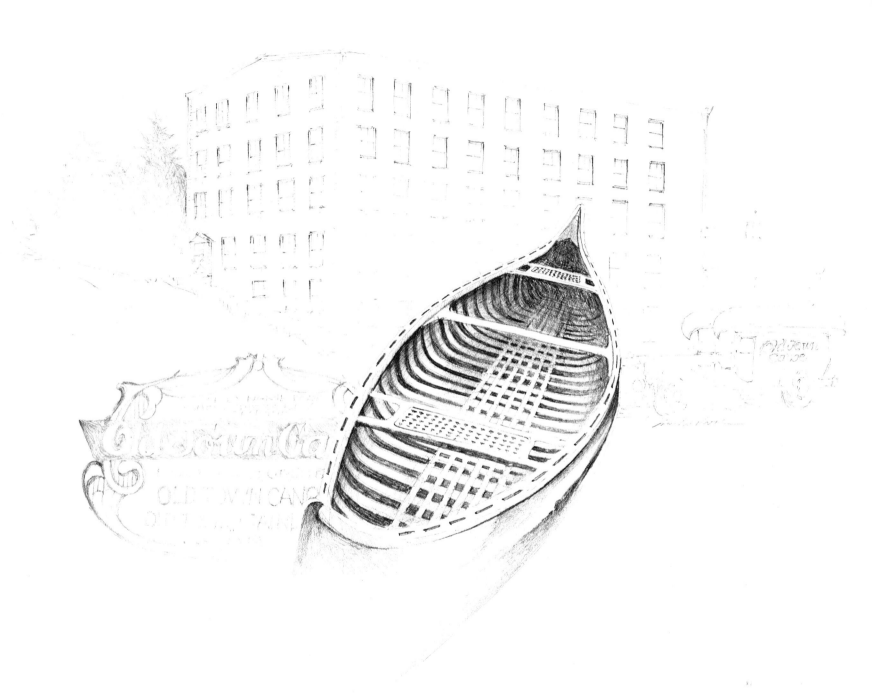

Penobscot River. It too has gone high-tech, producing hundreds of canoes made of synthetic materials in a century-old building. But down on one of the lower floors, well away from the odor of polyester, you can hear the tap of hammers and smell the cedar and oak as a few traditional wooden canoes are planked up, albeit with fiberglass coverings, no less elegant than the earlier ones the company made. Today Old Town Canoe is owned by a large corporation, but a small room lined with musty oak file drawers contains thousands of cards documenting every wooden canoe ever built there: "No. 16443 – 16′, trapper model, green [they were nearly always green], sold Mr. George Greenway 1936. Brought back by Mr. Ralph Greenway 1952, repair work. Restored 1962 as 50th wedding gift to Mr. and Mrs. George Greenway." This is not an actual account, but it is typical, and the accounts are often accompanied by a letter explaining the history and use of the purchased canoe.

A lot of boats go in and out of fashion, but no one can dispute the fact that the canoe is one of the most enduring designs. Aluminum, fiberglass, Kevlar, ABS rubber, wood epoxy, and who knows what else are used to build them today. Some canoes are punched out on presses in less time than it would take to strip bark off a tree, others appear in kit form, and still others are lovingly built in the traditional style (including birch bark) by enthusiastic amateurs and professionals.

Facing page: The Old Town Canoe Company in Old Town, Maine, has built canoes continuously since the 1890s. Although most canoes the company now produces are made from fiberglass and high-impact plastics, a section of the original factory is still used for manufacturing traditional wooden canoes.

CHAPTER THREE

GONE FISHING

*T*rout, salmon, pickerel, pike, bass — those flashing and seductively elusive swimmers that lead the sporting heart astray in spring and summer — have caused untold numbers of fishermen to head for the silvery lakes and rushing streams of the backcountry. Their pursuit is legendary, and the watercraft that became a part of the history of sport fishing are no less romantic.

By the early 1800s, as America began to prosper from hard work and a pioneering spirit, a small but growing number of sportsmen had the opportunity to post that classic "gone fishing" sign in their shop windows. For the first time, too, boats were being built that had little to do with earning a living — except for the guides who used them in a newly developed trade. Known as guide boats, these craft were rarely owned or operated by private sportsmen;

they were the working vehicles of the woodsmen. Hunters and trappers depended on these boats to make a living, for farming was barely an option in the North Woods. But around 1830, as early sportsmen arrived in the area, the local hunters began to see a more lucrative way to earn a wage. Using their tracking and waterway skills, they could offer the visiting sportsman the pleasures of the wilderness without the risk of perishing from or succumbing to the elements.

Master guides often had illustrious followings. Martin Moody of Tupper Lake, New York, guided luminaries such as Ralph Waldo Emerson, Louis Agassiz, and James Russell Lowell. Moody was an independent operator and required contract arrangements. There were two other guide classifications: the house guides, attached to the resort hotels (by 1890 there were few wilderness camps left; most establishments had running water and ballroom dancing); and the dockside "day trade" guides, held in contempt by the others as being hardly more than livery oarsmen.

The early guides were totally responsible for their charges, providing food as well as shelter, but by the turn of the century their services were in less demand. Thus began the decline of the trade — and the last days of the elegant guide boats, flashing in the sun as they made their way almost silently across a silver lake in pursuit of game fish.

The Adirondack Guide Boat

When we see the elegant and purposeful Adirondack guide boat, it is hard to imagine its clumsy beginnings. To look at a guide boat and a dory side by side, one would hardly guess they were related, but there was a natural evolution from one to the other. Below the waterline, both are double-enders, have flat bottoms, and are planked over frames. Form and use dictated that the guide boat would eventually be round-sided and light enough to carry.

Because early American records leave scanty details, the origin of the Adirondack guide boat is rather obscure. We do know that it came into existence around 1830, achieved its extraordinary perfection about 1900, then gradually fell into disuse. In spite of its short history, it became one of the most elegant and refined small craft ever to grace a waterway.

The first known Adirondack guide boat had a slender, flat, elliptical bottom board, with seven or eight clapboardlike planks on either side. There was a small transom above the waterline, and the boat was framed with natural crook spruce ribs. Around the 1870s the square stern evolved into a true double-ender — an interesting point of contrast with the later Rangeley Lakes boat, which started as a double-ender and later adapted a transom to accommodate the outboard motor.

The Adirondack was made largely of spruce and pine native to the North Woods. For the ribs, builders scoured the lumber-cutting sites for the big spruce roots that formed the natural curves needed, since steam-bending would weaken such a slender form. The narrow bottom plank would be set up on a form and

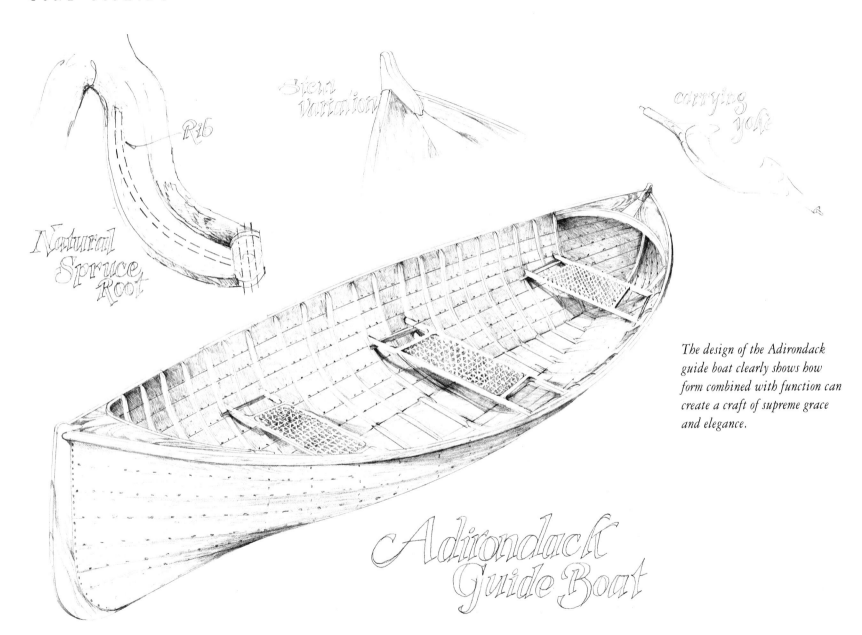

Rib

Natural Spruce Root

Stem Variation

carrying yoke

Adirondack Guide Boat

The design of the Adirondack guide boat clearly shows how form combined with function can create a craft of supreme grace and elegance.

the paired ribs attached. The real art of an Adirondack boat was the planking, and there were men who did little else. There were patterns for each plank, and to get the grain right, two or three pieces of wood often had to be scarfed together so that the grain would not distort. The edges of each plank, barely a quarter inch thick, were carefully beveled to make a perfect fit, and only a small amount of white lead was necessary for caulking. Consequently, few guide boats ever leaked. Planks were fastened with hundreds of small copper tacks, evenly spaced and carefully peened over on the inside to stay in place. Rails, inwales, and the small end decks became works of art, and the finished boat was like a finely tuned instrument.

In an effort to make the boat lighter, the planking was eventually refined so that the laps barely showed, resulting in a smooth skin that when varnished or properly painted was a pretty sight. Each subsequent builder seemed to refine some detail — stems became more graceful, entries finer, ribs more slender. The guide boat was fitted with a carved yoke amidships so that the craft could be easily carried across portages.

Among the many builders of the Adirondack guide boat, Henry Dwight Grant was perhaps the most prominent. He had been a guide for some twenty years when he turned to building the craft, and he had a distinguished career as a boatbuilder, sportsman, and guide. A learned, articulate man who owned a sawmill at Boonville, New York, Grant kept extraordinary tally boards, detailing length of hull, number of ribs, weight, costs of each boat, and information about clients. In 1880 a 12-footer brought $40; the same boat today would cost more than $2,000.

The Adirondack guide boat has made no wholesale return, nor has it been widely reproduced in fiberglass or aluminum. It is not a boat for the semiskilled to attempt to build, but instead demands the talents of devoted craftsmen. Two such master builders, Carl Hathaway and Ralph Morrow, teach guide boat building to willing and patient students at North Country Community College in Saranac Lake, New York. Care is taken to ensure that the boats are faithful reproductions, substituting only in cases where new materials or fastenings might help in the boats' longevity.

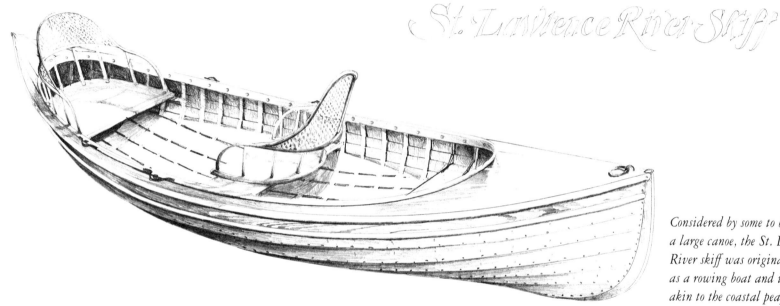

St. Lawrence River Skiff

Considered by some to be simply a large canoe, the St. Lawrence River skiff was originally built as a rowing boat and is actually akin to the coastal peapod.

Although the Adirondack is no longer abundant, its special qualities cannot be overlooked. It is a prime example of form and function equaling beauty.

The St. Lawrence River Skiff

We are told that water is a combination of two parts hydrogen and one part oxygen, with a little sodium thrown in for the ocean variety. But those are only the chemical properties of water; the bottom over which water passes and the part of the world through which it courses form its character — which in turn has dictated the great variety of boats that challenge its wiles.

The Adirondack guide boats were used almost exclusively on comparatively small inland lakes and were quite seaworthy for their given environment. But another fishing area that grew in popularity during the same period was the St. Lawrence Riverway – in particular, the area around Grindstone Island at Clayton, New York. Here, at the mouth of Lake Ontario, the conditions are more akin to open water. Even though there are legendary feats of oar-powered travel on the riverway, a boat for general use in these waters had to be more substantial and use more than the oarsman's strength to propel it. It had to be fast, too, as the guide business was highly competitive and the area to be covered was large. The Thousand Islands chain occupied a 50-mile stretch of water and was home to the best muskellunge fishing reported in North America during the late nineteenth century.

Although its properties were thought out carefully rather than evolving randomly, the St. Lawrence skiff was slow to develop. Some people consider the craft as simply a big canoe, but careful examination shows that the underwater body is more akin to the coastal peapod than to the Indian canoe. The average St. Lawrence boat is around 22 feet long, 4 feet wide, and more heavily built than the Adirondack boat, though similar in some aspects of construction.

The first one to be built is credited to Xavier Colon in 1868 and established the model that remains virtually unchanged today. Its primary function was as a guide's workboat, but the addition of a small centerboard and a sail (intended merely to make it faster getting to and from the fishing grounds) soon spawned a whole new use – racing. There was great rivalry between the guides of Gananoque, Ontario, and those of Clayton, and by 1880 annual regattas were being held. It was not long before the summer visitors took up the sport. What was remarkable about these sailing skiffs was that they could be sailed without rudders. They were originally built as rowing boats, but it was soon discovered that they could be made to come about by shifting one's weight in a certain manner. This was described in the August 1885 issue of *Century* magazine in the following manner:

> It sailed, with the aid of a small centerboard, by means of a large spritsail, the mast being stepped well forward when in use. The main peculiarity of the skiff under sail is that neither oar nor paddle is needed to guide it. Some persons help themselves come about on a fresh

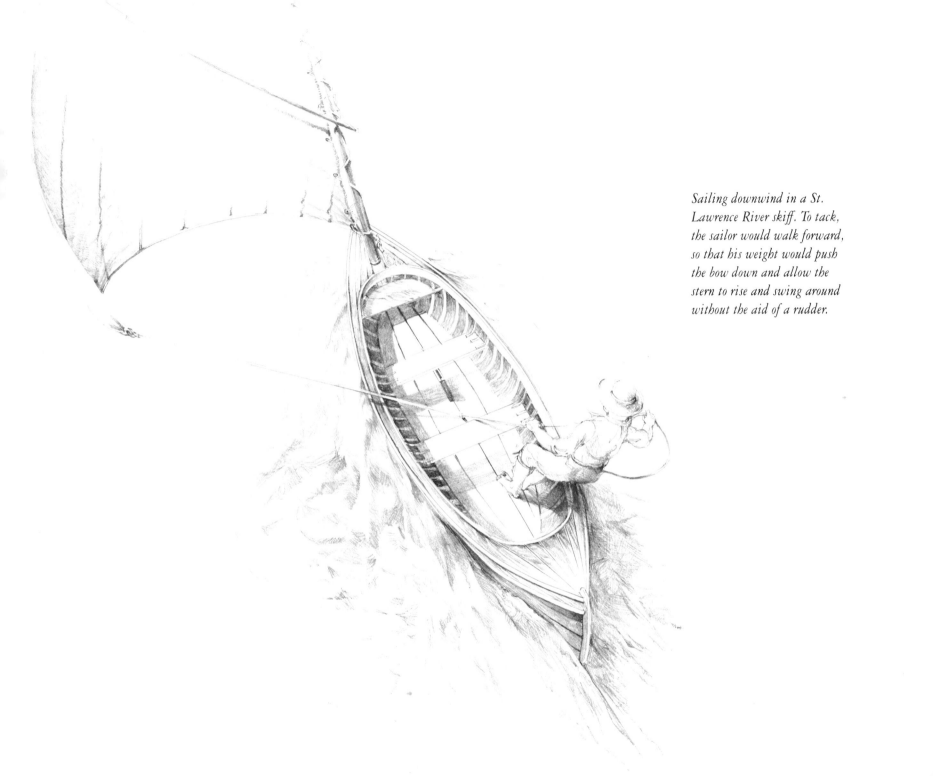

Sailing downwind in a St. Lawrence River skiff. To tack, the sailor would walk forward, so that his weight would push the bow down and allow the stern to rise and swing around without the aid of a rudder.

tack with the oars but this is not at all necessary, and is held in great scorn by a good sailor. The latter walks unconcernedly up and down his boat, pays her off the wind, or brings her up close-hauled as if by magic. The secret lies in distributing the weight of the sailor forward or backward. In order to bring the boat into the wind with the needed swiftness, he moves suddenly quite forward to the mast. This buries the bow of the boat, and the stern shaped like the bow rises up and is swung around by the wind. As soon as the sail shakes well in the wind, the skiff man runs fast, thus raising the bow which is helped along by the wind and depressing at the same time the stern.

It is curious to see how sensitive such a boat is to the weight of a man. Running free, he sits nearly aft. Should it be necessary to run directly before the wind he gets as far in the stern as possible; while to come up into the wind the reverse movement is made. First lessons in this unique boat deal severely with the shins of the novice and with the paint inside the boat, but a little practice gives mastery. In the skiff it is considered dangerous to make the mainsheet fast to the gunwale, because the boat is so long and narrow and shallow that it might easily be caught in one of the squalls that come with little warning down from the islands.

In 1887 the business established by Xavier Colon was taken over by Dr. A. Bain of Clayton, who was a devoted fan of the St. Lawrence skiff. Having good business sense, Dr. Bain was attuned to modern production practices and had a large three-story factory built — standardizing the manufacturing process. Although a good many skiffs were thus produced, the assembly line did not ignore quality. Like the Adirondack boat, the St. Lawrence skiff survives today largely in restored or revival versions, but it has never lost its appeal to those interested in "sail-dancing" a skiff on a breezy, challenging lake.

The Rangeley Lakes Boat

By the mid-1800s, when the resort areas of the Adirondacks and the St. Lawrence River were becoming "civilized," a group of anglers had discovered the abundant lakes in western Maine. And in 1868, at the junction of the Kennebago and Rangeley rivers, a place called Indian Rock became the home of the Oquossoc Anglers Association — one of the many true fishermen's camps for the sportsman who

The Rangeley Lakes Hotel in Rangeley, Maine, was a fashionable spa around the turn of the century, attracting sportsmen and their families as well as writers and artists.

wanted to get away from it all.

Needing boats for the club, the association commissioned Luther Tebbets, a local boatbuilder, to design a craft that would be suited for the waters on which it was to be used. The way the short, choppy waves on these lakes would fetch up determined the boat's length. It had to be just right so that the bow would not bury itself as it came off one wave, but instead would ride up over the next one. The result was a boat about 17 feet in length, double-ended, with a graceful sheer. It looked a little like the Adirondack boat but had construction similar to the St. Lawrence skiff. Unlike these other boats,

the Rangeley was not developed by the guides but was introduced to them by the fishermen who commissioned it.

By 1890 the fishing resort business had become the major industry of the region, and by that year there were five shops registered as builders. Most of the men built boats in the winter and served as fishing guides in the summer — taking their clients throughout the Rangeley Lakes area, including Oquossoc, Mooselookmeguntic, and other smaller lakes and streams nearby. It was not long before huge resort hotels sprang up as the fishermen began to bring their families along for vacations,

creating a demand for other entertainment. Since no one fished during the heat of the day, there were steamer trips around the lakes, lawn tennis and croquet games, and lavish dinners. Some of the Rangeley boats were even put to use as livery boats, so wives and children could enjoy the scenery.

By 1900 Rangeley was a fashionable spa, attracting artists and writers as well as sportsmen. Craftsmen such as flytiers, rod builders, and creel makers prospered, finding this an active center for their special wares. The Rangeley region was also lumber country, and by 1900 the railroad had replaced the wild and dangerous log drives as a better means of hauling logs to the mills in Rumford. Eventually, the lumber trains heading north began to carry private cars from Boston or New York — posh fishing, indeed.

Although many fishermen still preferred to "rough it" in camps in the outback, they also made time for their social life. Often they would hire a guide to row them to a party at another camp, perhaps 10 miles away, trusting their "driver" to get them home safely after the sportsmen had swapped fish stories and shared the strong spirits that always enhanced the size of their tales. Though obviously not designed for that express purpose, the Rangeley was a fast, stable, and easily rowed boat making such excursions possible.

Three Rangeley Boatbuilders

When we hear the word *tradition*, it evokes images of old pine, classic ornament, and the good old days when things were done with pride and love — not the hurried existence of today. There is no denying that the traditional period of American boatbuilding produced some wonderful classics, but at that time boatbuilding was just a job to be done, according to the standards of the day. Tradition refers to something that is recognized and permanent, but tradition does not mean dead or frozen in time. It goes on and ever shall. If a boat is created for a specific purpose today and becomes established, it joins the tradition. Or perhaps the craft has evolved, its earlier purpose having changed to suit a contemporary need.

The Rangeley has survived because it is well suited to modern recreational use, and thus

Facing page: This "gentleman fisherman," in formal sporting clothes of the day, makes a strike, while his hired expert, in less formal yet more practical attire, steadies the boat.

*Master boatbuilder Herb
Ellis inside his boat shop in
Rangeley, Maine.*

a demand for these boats continues. Profiled here are three builders – Herb Ellis, who is retired, began his career during the early guide boat trade; Bruce Malone re-creates the original Rangeley, using some finishing details of his own; and Bob Lincoln has adapted the traditional design to modern materials and methods of construction.

*   *   *

Herb Ellis lives a few miles outside of Rangeley; his boat shop is in a small building beside his house. Due to an illness he no longer builds, but his interest in boats is evident. Herb has worked as a carpenter and at many other trades over the years, but his main lifework has been with boats.

Herb built his boats well and in a clean, straightforward manner. He knew what they were going to be used for and how. His workmanship was sound but not fussy. He built his last Rangeley several years ago with his son, but the shop still looks as though the saws and hammers could buzz and ring at any moment; and as Herb picks up each tool or pattern, it seems as though he were still in the middle of a working day. Overhead and in corners is ready stock, cut and aged, and it is easy to imagine a well-dressed fisherman from fifty years ago coming here to pick up his new boat.

Herb explains how a Rangeley is built and why:

> Rangeleys have this wide, flat bottom board — that's why they're so stable. Have to be so's a fisherman can stand up in them and cast. This is mostly fly-fishing, you see, around here. They're fine-ended, though, so as to row easy. Sometimes it gets pretty rough out on the lakes — the mountains create this big downwind draft, and it can boil up some. Never heard of a Rangeley goin' over, though; you can just lie down in her and get to shore somewhere, safe.
>
> We set up these forms — patterns haven't changed but little over the years — and set up the bottom plank over the forms. We use good cedar — grows plenty around here. That's for the planks; the ribs are oak, and we have to get them down to Rumford. Once the bottom board is ready, I put on the planks — have to bevel them just right; that's the big job — and bed them in white lead; 'course you can't use that anymore. Then comes the nailing, lots of it. You have to get a rhythm with the hammer, but after a while I got so I could plank up a

Rangeley
Stool Seat

> boat in a long day.
>
> Now when you take the boat off the mold and turn it over, it's just a shell, wouldn't be much stronger than a paper boat. So we put in these oak ribs. They're soaked in hot water and then bent in. Used to be half round and prettier, but a lot of extra work, so one day I put in square ones because costs were getting higher. Had to make some changes like that, but we never compromised quality.
>
> The stem on a Rangeley just makes sense. You could have cut a rabbet in it, but then you'd have to fit each plank into that groove. This way we just run 'em on by and cut 'em off flush — put a stem piece on over that to protect the end.
>
> Now the seats used to be these round stool tops, pretty comfortable. But we couldn't get 16-inch clear pine anymore, and if I pieced

them they'd crack, and you know just where they'd pinch you. We just raised the thwarts and went with that.

About the time I bought my shop, the outboard motor came in. We started by just chopping off the stern of the double-ender and adding a little transom, but we found they'd squat under power, so we had to make the stern a little fuller. Just took a little four-horse to move her along nice, but some was in more of a hurry, so we built a few with higher sides and heavier to take up to an eight or ten [horsepower motor]. After that it doesn't make sense — too much vibration.

Most of the boats we painted — dark green on the outside and white in. If you wanted a varnished one, it was twice the work — each plank had to be picked perfect. I used a good quality trim paint, with a little drier. Modern yacht paint is too hard — won't stay in a seam. And when we had to repaint, the softer oil paint kind of chalked up so it'd be easier to sand her down for a new coat — after ten or twenty years you wouldn't have this heavy layer of paint flaking off.

I used to build fifteen or twenty boats a year. Not now, of course. My son and I built a few some years ago, but he isn't much interested — not that much call for them. Used to sell for three hundred; I think the last one went for around twelve hundred.

Bruce Malone, a traditional wooden-boat builder and restoration expert in Camden, Maine, is sensitive to the modern buyer's needs. Bruce takes the Rangeley's root values and adds his own special talents to refine its detail and enhance its beauty — but not at the cost of its original strength, seaworthiness, or purpose. Bruce is not the son of a boatbuilder but is a graduate engineer who decided that he felt most at home working with wood. He had built a few boats in his youth but now concentrates on boatbuilding full-time. Like his predecessors, he uses his skills for a variety of jobs, from restoration to repair. He is a realist who understands that there is not a steady market for Rangeley boats alone, no matter how beautiful and appealing they might be.

Bob Lincoln of Mount Desert, Maine, is a rowing enthusiast who saw a need to accomplish two things — adapt a traditional boat to meet the requirements of a growing recreational and competitive rowing market, and find a way to make such a boat affordable for the general public. To do this, he had to alter the Rangeley's construction and design. He replaced the traditional lapstrake planking with strip

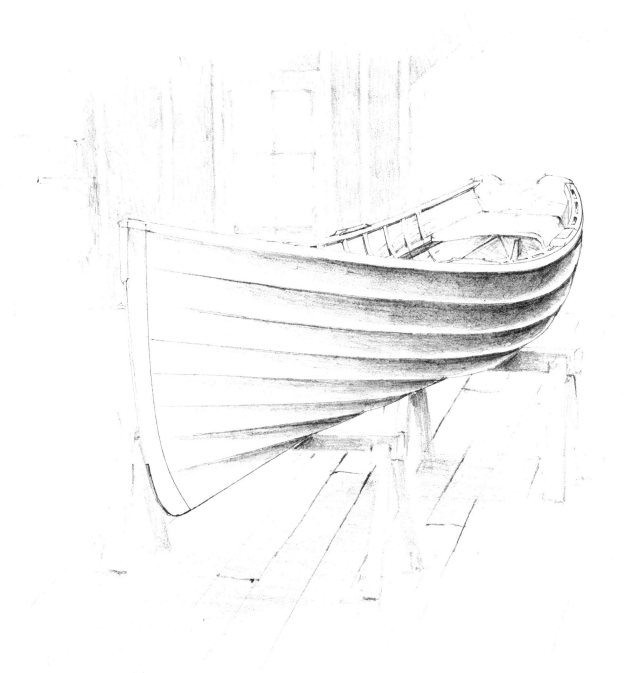

This Rangeley guide boat, built by Bruce Malone, is faithful to the spirit and tradition of the original craft.

*Bob Lincoln's adaptation of the
Rangeley produced a lively
competition boat.*

planking, which eliminated most of the internal framing and thus created a lighter yet incredibly strong hull. He also made the boat lighter by removing the Rangeley's several dozen ribs. Since an appreciable amount of time was saved by using these methods, costs could be cut. And by covering the hull with a thin layer of fiberglass, the wood surfaces were sealed and thus maintenance was reduced.

Since strip planking produces only smooth-sided boats, Bob also sought another means to build a modern wooden boat. He turned to a high-grade mahogany plywood, commonly known as Brynzeel, and added a special grooved edge so that the planks could be joined together tightly with epoxy. These planks do not swell or split like cedar, and the boat can still be assembled without framing – preserving the lightness of the strip boats.

Bob Lincoln's innovative methods have allowed him to turn out a greater volume of boats at a more competitive price. Along with his fiberglass version – still highly crafted and detailed with wood – Bob also offers a finely constructed wooden boat that appeals to the classic-minded buyer.

* * *

What has happened to the Rangeley serves as a good example of evolutionary tradition. In fact, were it not for the current state of the boat, the Rangeley might have passed into obscurity. As it is, boats based on the basic Rangeley design wind up in Alaska, Florida, and all points in between – places where they would have been unlikely to migrate on their own.

And so, even as it is being reshaped, the Rangeley boatbuilding tradition is carried on.

CHAPTER FOUR

THE LOBSTERMAN AND THE BOATBUILDER

*I*t's a warm summer morning at half tide in a shallow bay Down East. A young boy wades out among the rocks, poking among them with a short gaff hook. Soon he comes up with a lobster, which he tosses into a basket onshore, along with the twenty or thirty others he's already gathered. The lad is none too fond of the work, but his father won't do it, considering it beneath a serious fisherman's dignity. And while the catch is worth barely a penny a pound, it does boost the family income somewhat.

That plentiful cove is still there, but the lad and, later, his grandsons are long gone, as are the abundant crustaceans so easily gathered in the late eighteenth century. Like its companion delicacy the oyster, the critter once considered poor man's food has become anything but plentiful and cheap. The development of lobstering as an industry, however, has made it a way of life for New Englanders for more than a century. As the cosmopolitan taste for lobster expanded, so did the development of the boats that were needed to catch them — much to the joy, one supposes, of the young boys whose morning chores became men's work.

For a while lobsters were fished using wire baskets with bait suspended from the handles. These were lowered over the side of a skiff or rowboat in areas where the fishermen could see or sense the bottom. Eventually, the deep-water trap known today was developed, and the fishing began in earnest. Over a period of time, a wide variety of coastal watercraft was produced, progressing from small skiffs to modern high-powered 50- and 60-footers. While some of the boats were designed just for lobstering, many served a wider spectrum of

The earliest type of lobster trap, which was used in shallow waters.

The Moosabec Reach boat supplied the well-smack schooner with freshly caught fish and seafood, which was then transported to market.

fishing and transportation needs.

The Grand Banks dory (described in Chapter Nine) quickly became a popular coastal fishing boat because of its seaworthiness and ability to haul large amounts of gear and catch. But because the earliest lobstering was done close to shore, smaller and lighter craft also began to appear. This chapter focuses on the development of such boats in Maine, for the basic types that evolved there largely mirror the lobster boats used in other areas.

In the early 1800s, fishing for lobsters increased steadily, and southern areas were quickly fished out. Well-smack schooners began to move north, picking up cargo from lobstermen working out of small boats from Portland eastward. A well-smack was a large schooner with a "live well" in the middle for holding the catch and keeping it alive until reaching the markets in Boston and New York. (Since refrigeration was not available at this time, the only way to keep fish and seafood fresh was by salting it down or keeping it on ice or in salt water.) Along the Maine coast, two small boats were commonly used as suppliers to these dealers — the reach boat from "down

Jonesport way" and the peapod from "over to Deer Isle."

Any small boat would work alongshore, and almost any type that was handy was used. But people who work on the water constantly try to improve the efficiency of their boats and develop craft that seem better suited to the trade and the local conditions in which they work. The Moosabec Reach boat was so named for the long tidal reaches along which it worked. It was generally 14 to 16 feet in length, about 4 feet in beam, and constructed of cedar planking over steam-bent oak ribs. It had a wide, nearly flat bottom for load-carrying and stability, with low sides to ease hauling traps. It was generally rowed, though sometimes it was fitted with a small spritsail for a speedier trip home on a favorable breeze. Few originals are still around, and few are made today.

*   *   *

Of all the small rowing and sailing craft along the Maine coast, perhaps the best known is the peapod (whose name comes from its shape), which has a reputation for extreme

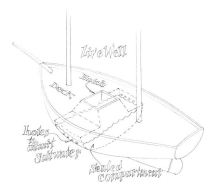

Location of the live well in a typical well-smack schooner.

Maine Peapod

seaworthiness. One story tells of two lobstermen caught in a gale in their peapod. A well-smack schooner, itself being badly thrown about by the storm, came upon the pair and offered to take them aboard. The two men declined, saying they felt safer in the sturdy little double-ender.

The peapod resembles a stout canoe but has higher sides and a wide bottom. Whether it is a direct descendant of the canoe is not known, although the Penobscot Indians did build some very substantial sea canoes. While the peapod did not become established as a general design in Penobscot Bay until about 1870, some double-enders had been built on the coast since at least 1840.

Peapods average 15 feet and are exactly alike (or nearly so) at both ends. Some have relatively flat bottoms amidships, and some have more deadrise or a V shape, but all have sharp (pointed) entry/exit at the ends, which allows a smooth flow of water around the hull for easy rowing, as well as for sliding through rough seas. Some are built with a shallow keel running the length of the boat to help it track and sail better, and often they are equipped with centerboards for going to windward. Peapods are

built of thin cedar planks, carvel or lapstrake, over bent-oak or hard-pine ribs. The bottom board or keel is always oak to withstand the rough grounding while beaching over the rocky shores of Maine.

Though small in size, the peapod makes a steady working platform, ideal for hauling lobster traps. You can stand with your weight largely on the rail without capsizing, and when loaded, the boat is not much lower in the water than when empty. The peapod's use for lobstering began to wane in the late 1800s as the demand for larger catches increased and the alongshore fishing grounds thinned out. But its design qualities have made it attractive today as a recreational boat – some built as restoration craft in exactly the same manner as in the past, and others with modified hulls to make them lighter and faster rowing and sailing craft.

Around 1880 a class of small sailing sloops worked by lobstermen began to appear on Muscongus Bay. Over time this boat with humble working origins blossomed into one of the most handsome pleasure yachts around. Form followed function, and in the case of the Muscongus sloop boat, that form was graceful

Facing page: With special tall oarlocks, a peapod could be rowed while standing up and facing forward — a special advantage to a lobsterman tending his traps.

indeed. Here is a vessel that had to be capable of being handled by one man, as there was not enough profit in lobstering (at one or two cents a pound) to support a paid hand. The rig had to be balanced so that the fisherman could leave it untended long enough to haul in his traps. Sometimes he would have a comblike affair across the after end of the cockpit so he could set the tiller in such a manner as to let the boat sail in a slow circle while he worked. The boat had a large, deep cockpit for stowing gear and the catch, with a small cuddy, or cabin, way forward in case of foul weather.

The outstanding feature of the Muscongus sloop boat is the hull. It has a wide beam amidships with a sharp turn to the bilge (sharp angle where the bottom meets the sides) for stability. The bow is high to punch through heavy seas, while the stern is quite low to make working over the sides easier. The underbody is very trim to make it faster, with a long, straight, deep keel and sufficient ballast to keep the boat upright in a blow. Even with all these features, the first models were not as "eye sweet" as the later ones, for builders could not long resist adding a nicer sheer and a prettier transom and

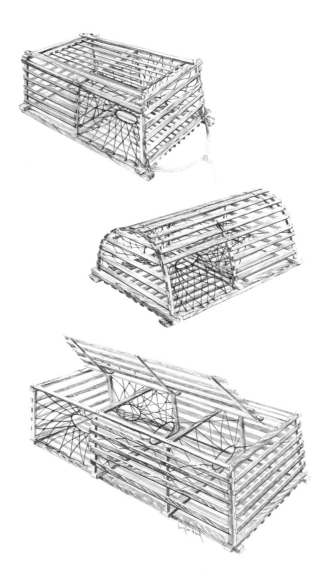

Deep-water lobster traps. Attracted to the bait inside, a lobster enters through the openings in the mesh, but cannot get back out because of the shape of the netting.

bow to a hull that seemed to have inborn grace, despite its utilitarian requirements.

While it is true that many fishermen also were competent boatbuilders, the sloop boat did much to further the trade of boatbuilding on the coast of Maine. The earliest Muscongus boats ran 20 feet or so — hardly a backyard project. Their elegant curved transoms, S-shaped frames, and tricky planking runs required more and more sophisticated skills.

As power came into use, a few lobstermen tried installing engines on the boat, but it did not adapt well; it was too sharp forward to drive well at faster speeds. Were it not for a new group of people beginning to enjoy the coast of Maine, the boat might have vanished. By 1920, however, the summer tourist trade was in full flower, and yachtsmen began buying up the retired Muscongus boats and turning them into painted and polished beauties.

The Muscongus boat of the 1890s evolved into the Friendship sloop of today. Down in the thriving lobster port of Friendship, Maine, it is generally acknowledged that Wilbur Morse built the first contemporary sloop. Other builders were active in the bay around 1900,

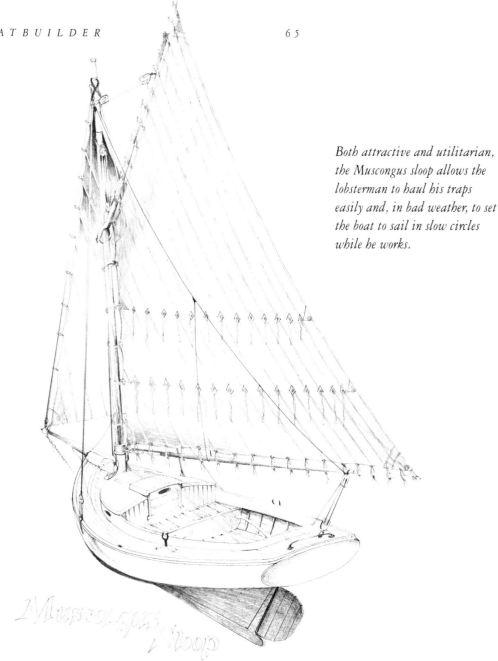

Both attractive and utilitarian, the Muscongus sloop allows the lobsterman to haul his traps easily and, in bad weather, to set the boat to sail in slow circles while he works.

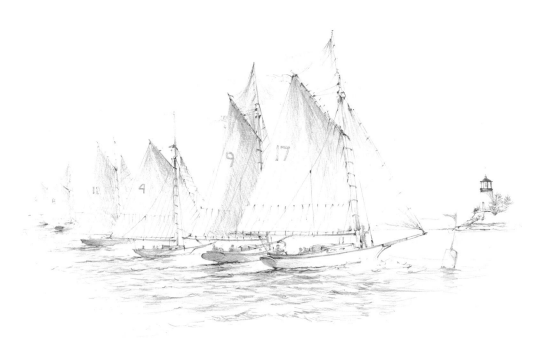

The Friendship Sloop Society regatta is held each summer in Boothbay Harbor, Maine. Some boats in the competition are more than eighty years old.

Started in 1961 by Bernard MacKenzie after he won a yacht club race in Boston Harbor with *Voyager,* the society lists more than three hundred boats in its registry, with more than fifty in Class A (boats built before 1920) still sailing. The Friendship Sloop Society holds an annual regatta each July. Until recently the regatta was held in Friendship Harbor, but due to its popularity, it has moved to Boothbay Harbor, which can accommodate larger crowds.

America's Cup racing may be world-class impressive, the Tall Ships majestic and awe inspiring because of their size, but few spectator events can rival the moment when fifty or so lovely gaff-rigged Friendships start across the line. The race is an enduring spectacle, and even though the competition is keen among certain long-standing rivals, this is also a family event. Many boats finish long after the winners are ashore, but everyone enjoys his or her time on the water.

however, and thus the claim is sometimes disputed.

The Morse boats were classics, though, and when the first race of the Friendship Sloop Society took place, at the vanguard was *Voyager,* built in 1906. The society today is a remarkable tribute to traditional watercraft, as well as a fine example of the transitional use of such vessels.

The Friendship is a true survivor. New ones are available today in both fiberglass and wood, some simple and some fancy, but few builders have messed with the design, even after nearly a century.

Sometimes a boat such as the Friendship survives in its original form; other times it evolves from one era to the next, a new use growing out of a former one. Such is the case of the Hampton. In the 1880s, it was a double-ended ketch-rigged sailing boat that was quite fast and, because of its fishing use, a steady and capable workboat. As the need arose to carry more gear, a flat transom and wider stern were added – giving it a form suitable to power well before power was available. When an engine was added (around 1900), the long, straight keel still proved advantageous. Although the exact origin of many boats is either disputed or obscure, there is no doubt that the design of the Hampton had a direct influence on the modern lobster boat.

The Hampton introduced another chapter in small craft building – strip planking. The strip-built boat has a strong, lightweight hull of considerable durability. Given the demands engine power makes on a hull, this is an important factor. The powered Hampton is still around, being built today for recreational use by Richard Pulsifer on Casco Bay. (Pulsifer's Hampton is described in Chapter Nine.)

A double-ended Hampton with strip planking.

*The Knox Marine make-and-
break single-cylinder engine is
about as basic as an engine can
be. This 4-horsepower model is
put into reverse by stopping the
engine and spinning the flywheel
in the opposite direction.*

When we think of power today, we
generally think of the small but highly efficient
engines that move boats along at 25 knots or so.
But the first marine engines were very heavy and
slow, such as the 1904 Knox Marine make-and-
break 1½-horsepower motor, a typical
installation in an early Hampton boat. The
steady 4 or 5 knots of speed it delivered were a
boon to the lobsterman and represented another
advance in the industry – a better edge of safety.
A story is told of a fisherman whose lobster
sloop became becalmed. He threw a quarter
overboard, hoping for wind. A squall came up,
and the boat was swamped – a total loss – and
when the bedraggled fisherman managed to get
ashore, he allowed as how he should have asked
only for a dime's worth. Classic Maine humor to
be sure, but it points out the advantages of
power, since lobstering is not a fair-weather
trade.

The engine progressed along with boat
design, and by the 1920s 4-cylinder, 20- and
25-horsepower units were in common use. The
Hampton was a little small for this increase and
tended to get rather wet punching through the
spray. At first a canvas dodger was added to

keep both engine and occupant dry, then a small
shelter cabin was tried. Soon, however, the boat
got broader and longer, and the modern boat
design began to evolve.

In most areas where boatbuilding plays a
prominent role, both pride and rivalry are
evident in the designs. Around Jonesport-Beals
Island heated local debate still surfaces from
time to time as to who was the father of the
Down East version of the lobster boat. The truth
probably is that it had many fathers, all of
whom learned from each other, whether they
admitted it or not. Certainly one of the most
prominent was Will Frost – a transplanted
"Novi" from Digby, Nova Scotia. In 1912 he
built a narrow powerboat that was about twice
as fast as the local variety. Frost later produced
the famous *Redwing,* a sleek craft with a 4-
cylinder engine and a rounded, raked stern
known as a torpedo stern. Some say that stern
style was the invention of Eddie Kelley, who one
day was towing a small model for a boat he
planned to build. When it inadvertently turned
upside down, he found it had less resistance to
the water that way, and thus the reverse transom
was born. The name itself comes from the early

Alvin Beal, dean of the Beals Island boatbuilders, in his younger days, sitting in his first lobster boat — a torpedo-stern model.

style of naval destroyers, leading to further speculation about the origin of the design.

As attractive as this design was, it presented tricky planking problems, and as time was money, the square stern soon became the standard. It was easier to build and provided a wider platform for hauling or stacking traps.

Today there are few places where the wooden workboat survives in its original form. But Jonesport-Beals Island is one of those isolated spots where both the pace of life and the craft of boatbuilding remain somewhat the same as they have for the past half century. There are fewer boat shops now, but the demand for solid wooden lobster boats continues — enough so that some builders are kept busy year-round. The advent of fiberglass seemed for a while to forebode the end of the Jonesport shop, but although good quality fiberglass boats have found their place in the industry, many

fishermen have come back to wood.

It's not the demand, however, that threatens the shops; it's supply and sociology. Getting good wood is more difficult now, as most cedar goes for house siding, and making the long, straight oak timbers just right is too much bother for most mills, which can sell thousands of board feet to the housing industry. Lobster-boat building has always been an apprenticed craft, since boats are built by eye and experience, but the younger generation is being lured away. The electronic media have sparked the vision of better rewards for less work outside the isolated communities of Jonesport-Beals Island. Lovely as the scenery is, one does have to love the sea, long winters, and basketball to be content there.

Lobster-boat building is a straightforward type of work. The boats are inherently handsome but not fussy, constructed by one or two men working a long day in a modest tarpaper-and-plank building that seems to belie the boatbuilder's sense of craftsmanship. Each builder has his own style, his own set of well-used molds, and his own views on the finer points of design. Most also are related, being either an Alley or a Beals.

The towns have fourteen churches altogether and no bars — though nobody has anything against a beer or a warm bit of whiskey on a cold day. They come alive around the Fourth of July, when the World's Fastest Lobster Boat Race is held along the Moosabec Reach, starting under the Jonesport-Beals Island Bridge. The competition is fierce. Engines get tuned as hot as they'll stand (Lincolns and Chevys are favorites), boats get painted, families bring picnics, and the waters churn with four or five boats at a time reaching 40 to 50 miles per hour. The races provide enough excitement to last all winter, when discussions are fueled by speculation as to why one boat lost or whether another might have cheated in order to win. Some boats have even been built just to race, never having hauled a single trap in their days, though this isn't fancied by the locals.

The building of a modern wooden lobster boat is an example of both sound, practical craftsmanship and the Yankee work ethic. In the many shops Down East, one finds a slow, steady pace and little unnecessary conversation (unless the builder stops for a "jaw," a legitimate

Facing page: In shops with only basic equipment yet experienced craftsmen, sturdy, graceful lobster boats can be constructed in just about two months.

diversion). Given this serenity, it may seem surprising that a large 30-footer often emerges from the shop in less than two months. Many of us who build for a hobby have labored far longer over a little skiff, as we tend to fuss and fiddle with the finish and extras characteristic of pleasure craft. Few of us are used to the workaday approach to boatbuilding born of generations of hard work. What the men of Beals Island do with simple tools and little wasted motion is not just an acquired skill, it is an attitude about the job to be done. They have done it for so long that each move is instinctive.

Living so close to the sea, often lobstering himself in the summer, each builder is fused with his art. Although he uses his skill to earn a living on or from the water, the Beals Islander produces his own "poetry." First there is the simple, clean efficiency of the boat, finished with care if not polish, moving just right through the water. Then there is the unspoken pride of the builder in his work and the fisherman in his craft, along with a damn fine appreciation of a good sunrise and sunset, usually seen by both the builder and the lobsterman in the course of the same working day.

The history of the lobster boat and the industry is well documented in a permanent exhibit titled "Lobstering and the Maine Coast" at the Maine Maritime Museum in Bath, Maine. It includes an indoor display of all the boats covered in this chapter, plus an excellent film, written and narrated by E.B. White, that portrays a day in the life of a lobsterman.

Facing page: Normally a quiet fishing community, the Jonesport-Beals Island area comes alive every Fourth of July, as it hosts the World's Fastest Lobster Boat Race along Moosabec Reach.

CHAPTER FIVE

BUGEYES,
TONGERS,
AND
WATERMEN

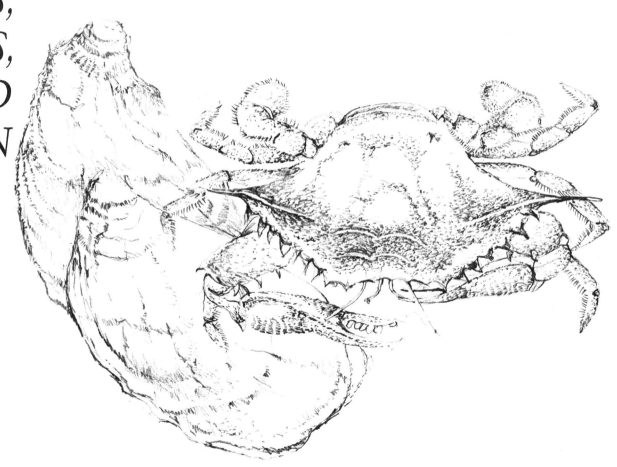

Chesapeake Bay is one of America's most intriguing waterways. Virtually open ocean at the mouth, it winds its way up to the Potomac River via countless small inlets and islands, snaking and meadering up dozens of creeks and so shallow in spots one could nearly walk from point to point. It is a major scene of American history; of naval encounters, Indian wars, trading, and fishing. The shallow bottom is a natural breeding ground for oysters, called "erst'rs" by the native watermen and still harvested under sail by graceful but utilitarian skipjacks "going drudgin'."

Oyster fishing has been a major factor on the bay since before the colonists settled here in the early 1600s. The Indians first built dugout canoes along the banks of the Choptank River in Chesapeake Bay, though not exclusively for fishing, as the Chesapeake's "roads" were its waterways — the only practical way to get around. Though the Indians' tools and skills were limited to stone axes and the use of fire to hollow out logs, many of their dugouts were as long as 40 feet, carrying twenty-five paddlers. When the colonists arrived, at first they bought Indian dugouts for transportation and fishing, but as oysters became a market product as well as a staple, they needed larger boats. With better steel implements and imported boatbuilding knowledge, they soon found a means of joining two logs together with locust pins to form a wider, more stable craft capable of carrying larger loads.

Market demands influenced design again, and the log canoes developed rapidly. Top logs were added for higher sides, and soon sails were employed to help get the oysters to market more quickly. The oysters were harvested from the

These oyster tongs are used to scoop up oysters from the shallow, sandy bottom of the oyster bed and haul them aboard the boat.

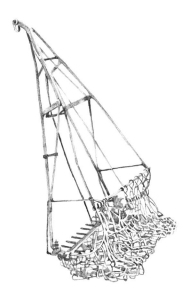

The oyster dredge, a heavy but efficient device, is dragged along the oyster bed, raking the catch into its net.

boats by means of long wooden tongs that allowed fishermen to scoop up the shells in the shallows. By 1800 the New England oyster fisheries had developed a large metal dredge that could be dragged along the bottom behind a schooner for faster harvesting. However, this method quickly depleted the local oyster beds, so the Maryland and Virginia legislatures passed laws forbidding the use of dredges. Restricted to tong fishing, the watermen had to develop even larger boats to eliminate the middlemen and take their catches directly to the markets in Baltimore and Annapolis. Thus the log canoe evolved further into a form called a Brogan, about 35 feet long with two sharply raking masts, and the Brogan evolved into the bugeye ketch — 50 feet on deck, built up with from seven to nine logs, with fully planked sides and a powerful sail plan to allow the boat to haul the dredges in all weather.

The origin of boat names is often lost in legend and lack of documented history. Some say the bugeye was named for the Scottish Buckeye schooner, since a large number of Scots settled in the bay area. Others claim it was for the eyes often painted on either side of the bow

to "watch" for shallows. In any case the bugeye had begun its long reign on the bay by 1820, being rivaled only in later years by the single-masted skipjack.

No two bugeyes were built alike, even by the same builder. Usually they were constructed without drawn plans (as were most working craft) — just a small model and the shipwright's accumulated experience. The important things were strength and efficiency, though few if any builders remained unconscious of design, and the hulls of the bugeyes were usually visually appealing.

The rig is a racy and romantic sight — both masts are raked (or tipped) back about 15 degrees, but the reason is strictly functional. With the masts set back in this fashion, the center of effort (drive) remains the same whether the sails are set full for light airs or reefed down for heavy weather. This is an important factor, as conditions change rapidly in the broad shallows of the oyster grounds and the work must continue regardless of weather.

Bugeyes, like all utilitarian vessels, were worked hard and there was little time or money for any but absolutely necessary maintenance;

A Brogan ketch, the earliest sailing oyster boat, and single-log dugouts with fishermen tonging for oysters.

most examples of the breed simply rotted away in the backwaters, after an average life span of about twenty years. Therefore, the survival of the *Edna B. Lockwood,* the only example still sailing today, is fortunate. Her builder was John B. Harrison, who was regarded as perhaps the finest shipwright on the bay in 1888, when the contract for the *Lockwood* was signed.

Harrison had gone to work with his father on Tilghman Island at the age of twelve. At seventeen he built his first boat, the 49-foot bugeye *Mary L. Cooper.* By 1889, not yet twenty-five, he had built five bugeyes, and in that year he launched his sixth and seventh, including the *Lockwood*. During his career he built a total of eighteen bugeyes and about two hundred other small boats. He was a hard driver, a fair but tough boss, and remains a legend on Tilghman Island today. His racing canoes built in later years were legendary for

To rough out a small five-log Brogan, the builder would connect the logs at one end with long iron pins and then hew the general shape with an adze.

their grace and craftsmanship, and his *Jay Dee* and *Flying Cloud* are considered the fastest ever sailed.

Work on the *Lockwood* started in the fall of 1888 at the Harrison yard, which, like all other Chesapeake shipyards, was little more than a level place on a creek, with perhaps a shed for tools. The total sail-away cost of the boat was to be about $2,200, at a time when wages averaged 15 cents an hour. The bottom logs,

nine in all, were selected and hewn out with adzes to the desired shape — first upside down according to the builder's model, then turned over while the inside was hollowed out. The pieces were then joined with long iron drift pins. Frames were set up on the top logs, and the sides were planked and fastened at the ends to stem and stern pieces. The deck planks were laid down straight fore and aft, then caulked and tarred. A rail was added with scuppers, through which the water that washed aboard could drain.

The masts were massive, cut from local pine heartwood. A cuddy was added forward, and seven months from the time the first log chips flew, the *Lockwood* was ready to be launched, the whole boat having been built by only three or four men.

Her owner, Daniel Haddaway, put her to work straightaway, with little ceremony wasted on sea trials. The *Lockwood* carried two dredges, port and starboard. When on an oyster bed, the dredges would be lowered over the side and dragged along the bottom by sail power. Care had to be taken to achieve the right speed: at less than 2 knots, the dredges would dig in and

At work on the Edna B. Lockwood. *It took about seven months to complete construction on this bugeye.*

anchor the boat; but at a speed of more than 3 or 4 knots, the scoops would miss the oysters. At the end of each tack the dredges would be hauled in and the oysters dumped on deck for sorting. The whole operation required great skill on the part of the skipper, and the strength and endurance of the crew, as everything was muscle powered and allowed no time for staring at the scenery.

A working week for an oysterman usually began before daylight on Monday and involved dredging, sorting, and storing the marketable oysters — over and over until dark, when the bugeye would seek shelter in the nearest creek for the night. The six or seven men would squeeze into the small cuddy around the stove for dinner, sleeping as best they could on very small berths. This would continue all week, or until the holds were full. In foul winter weather, with freezing spray and frequent squalls, it was hard and often dangerous work. With full holds the *Lockwood* would be so deep in the water that the waves sloshed over her decks, and in this cumbersome fashion she would make her way up the bay for Baltimore, trying for the utmost speed, as the first boats in got the best prices.

Then came the run for home — with luck on Saturday afternoon, or if the winds did not favor them, just in time to start over again on Monday. Hardship, injury, and loss of life were taken for granted in this hard winter trade, yet it tempered the men, who stood it with grace.

By spring the oystering was finished, but not the boat's work. Cleaned up and with the covering boards removed from the hatches, the *Lockwood* became a cargo and passenger boat. With just captain and cabin boy for crew, she would haul what she could — grain, lumber, watermelons, tomatoes, cattle, horses — acting as the waterborne trucking company of the day.

In 1892 the *Lockwood* changed hands. She continued working the oyster trade under various owners until 1967 — an unprecedented life span for a dredger. However, after seventy-eight years of service she was run-down: Patches had been put upon patches, and it seemed that she would end up on the same dry creek bed as her long-deceased sister ships. Fortunately, in 1967, John Kimberly bought her and took her to Captain Jim Richardson on the Choptank River. Richardson fixed her up enough so that she could be sailed as a pleasure craft.

The *Lockwood*'s last owner donated her to the Chesapeake Bay Maritime Museum at St. Michaels, Maryland, with the stipulation that she be preserved and displayed. The bugeye could have been hauled ashore, propped up, and painted to create a static exhibit, but instead she was restored to demonstrate her sailing grace. The restoration actually was more a re-creation, however, as all that could be saved of the original were the massive rough-hewn logs of the hull. Everything else had to be remade from scratch, and the task fell to veteran Tilghman Island boatbuilder Maynard Lowery. With professional expertise and a lot of volunteer labor, the "new" *Lockwood* was launched in 1979. It was every bit the boat the old bugeye had been, in spirit if not in substance, and was ready for another hundred years of service.

Another log canoe was working the bay at the same time as the bugeye and the later skipjack — either tonging for oysters or fishing for crabs. Being narrower and lighter, this boat was fairly fast, even under a working rig. Made up of pinned-together bottom logs just as the larger bugeyes were, she had a centerboard to counteract leeway and a long, graceful "false"

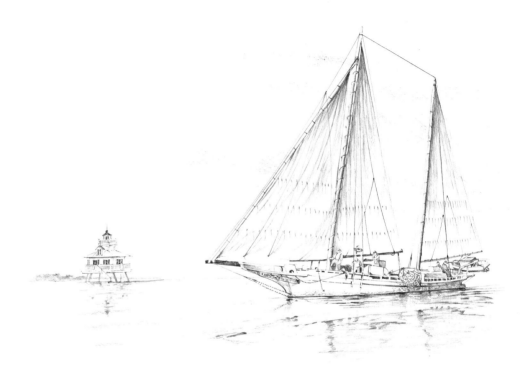

bow with a sprit to carry bigger headsails. On Sundays during the mid-1800s the rig might be unshipped and larger sails used to race on the Miles, Chester, and Tred Avon rivers. This was a workingman's sport, well fueled by pride, rivalry, and no doubt a goodly ration of rum.

With the advent of the gasoline engine

The Lockwood *heading out for a day's work. In the background is a "spider" lighthouse, so named for the stilt-like legs on which it stands.*

around 1900, tonging under sail declined, and with it the log canoe; from 1903 to 1933 not a one was built. Yachtsmen, however, became enamored of the design and commissioned Harrison to build two new and very fast canoes – the above mentioned *Jay Dee* and *Flying Cloud*. Others followed suit, and canoe racing was reborn, financed perhaps by the wealthy, but often crewed and certainly enjoyed by the watermen.

These fast canoes carried rigs that would have been insane to use on a workboat. To try (not always successfully) to keep from capsizing, the crew would hike out on several springboards set on the windward side. Racing these overcanvased boats could be wild and exhilarating. During one race on a Harrison boat with the builder aboard, the crew got behind in a bit of light air and urged Harrison to let them put up the square sails. He advised against it, cautioning that a puff could come up and bury their bow, but they persisted. As soon as the sails went up, a squall hit. Some of the crew panicked and asked him to take off sail, but he said, "Never – let the wind blow 'em off." When they hit the beach downriver, she went

five full boat lengths up onshore.

Both original and reproduction racing log canoes can still be seen in action. Every year in St. Michaels, Maryland, a maritime regatta is held during the summer.

By the late 1880s another type of oyster workboat – the skipjack – began to appear on the Chesapeake Bay. Though massive in construction like the bugeye, it was easier and cheaper to build, being a completely planked boat. The first skipjacks were relatively small – 32 feet or so on deck. They had a shallow V bottom, with herringbone planking over a very heavy frame and atop a large skeg. The boats were usually built of the heartwood of old loblolly pine, with white oak used for the centerboard, skeg, and rudder.

The rig of the skipjack is on a single mast raked well aft, with a boom extending back beyond the stern and a single large jib, often fixed on its own boom to be self-tacking since the men on deck are usually busy with dredging and sorting. The skipjack is possibly the most overbuilt workboat in modern history – meant to take the strains of the massive rig in midwinter and to last more than fifty years. A

Facing page: Both original and reproduction racing log canoes compete in the maritime regatta held each summer in St. Michaels, Maryland.

powered skiff is carried on the stern to push the boat home in calm weather, and donkey engines are used to haul up the heavy dredges on deck but not to power the boat itself.

Dredging under sail with a skipjack is similar to the practice used with the bugeye – it is a precise sort of ballet managed gracefully for such a ponderous rig. Since more than one boat is usually working an area at the same time, a skipper had better be alert, for if he misses a tack and comes about too high, another captain will not hesitate to cut under his bow and make the dredge. Present Maryland law still forbids dredging under power, with the exception of one day a week at the skipper's option to compensate for light air. The fleet still sails the bay – around thirty-five boats remain at last count, but only one or two of them have been built in recent years. It is the last of the working sail in America, and its future is uncertain; the old boats are gradually retiring, having served in some cases well beyond their fifty years, and new ones are too expensive to build. Many skipjack yachts have been built, however, so the type is secure, and races for both working skipjacks and skipjack yachts are held each summer. But

something magnificent, even if representative of a demanding way of life, will pass from the bay the day the last skipjack comes ashore.

Anyone who has enjoyed a dozen fresh-shucked oysters, a bucket of steamed crabs, or a plate of perfectly prepared Maryland crab cakes can readily understand the preoccupation with fishing. Everybody, down to the smallest child with a bit of bait on a crab line, "works the bay" at one time or another. While the bigger boats are out dredging, tongers are working their shallows, crab potters are checking their traps, and everyone seems ready to sell – wholesale or retail. There also seems to be a special boat for every level of fishing.

Prior to the advent of the larger skipjacks, just before the turn of the century, flat- and V-bottomed skiffs and sloops were common in oystering, crabbing, waterfowling, and transportation. The Hampton (Virginia) flattie evolved after the Civil War and seemed to be the forerunner of the skipjack. At 27 feet, it had a wide, flat bottom that gradually became a shallow V as it reached the transom and was fitted with a deep skeg and a centerboard. The rig was a gaff mainsail and small jib. There was

Chesapeake Bay Skipjack

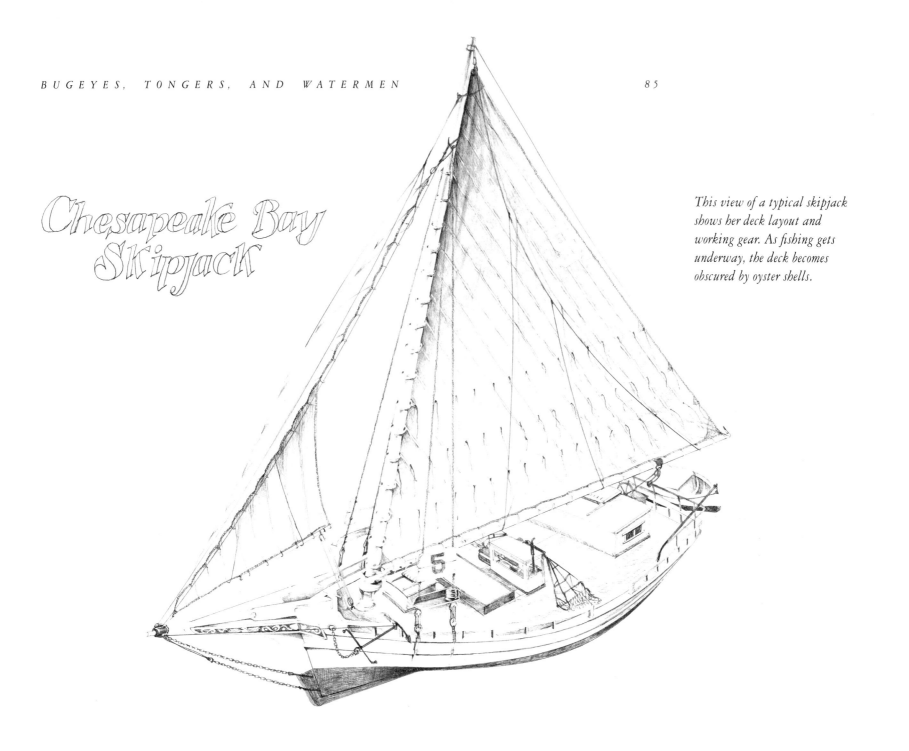

This view of a typical skipjack shows her deck layout and working gear. As fishing gets underway, the deck becomes obscured by oyster shells.

Hampton Flattie   *Stick-up Skiff*   *Chincoteague Skiff*

Shallow-water bay boats share similar characteristics: stability, ease of construction, and generous load-carrying capacity.

Facing page: The tuck-stern tonger – an early sailing model that was later converted to power. Contemporary powered tongers have wider, squared sterns.

a very small cuddy forward, as the boat was mostly daysailed. Flat-bottomed boats have always had a reputation for being stable, but they are often slow when loaded or on a tack. Local ingenuity soon led to the deadrise V sections aft, which, because the load was forward, made the boat quicker in maneuvering without affecting stability. This form seems to have influenced nearly all Chesapeake boats, as they tend to have both a lot of rocker and

deadrise aft. The flattie has not endured as a type because of its low freeboard and there being no way to alter this part of its design without ruining the boat's lines. Only a few have been built as pleasure craft.

Another small flattie that was seen on the Eastern Shore around 1860 was the 17-foot stick-up skiff. An open boat for crabbing and tonging, it had an unusual sail plan: A sprit-rigged main was raked well aft, with a curious

Not all traditionally based boats move along at a sedate 4 knots; the modern garvey, descendant of a sailing type, can do a steady 25 to 30 knots under power.

jib set on its own shorter mast up in the bow, raking forward of the boat. As strange as this looked, it was quite efficient, as the jib was always perfectly trimmed and provided power to windward.

Soon the flattie gave way to the more efficient V-bottomed, cat-rigged tonging skiff of about 20 feet that appeared around 1890. The most extreme version of this hull form was the ketch-rigged Chincoteague skiff, with wide flaring sides and a handsome profile. This boat was understandably fast and was still in use as late as 1950. It was replaced gradually by the sailing garvey — a wider hulled V-bottomed boat with a square bow — harbinger of powerboats to come.

With power came even further modifications of design. The tongers had their own special boats, very long and narrow launches with tuck-stern aft — suitable for sailing the shallows and stable enough for the short choppy seas. When power was introduced around 1915, the tonger was modified to have a broader stern, but it has retained its length for a steady work platform, as the fishermen have to stand on the rail to work the long and cumbersome tongs. These are certainly unusual looking boats, but they have their own charm and seem to be the perfect craft for their trade.

The garvey, descendant of the sailing garvey, seems to have been made for the outboard engine. As it developed from the sailing model, the bottom was widened and the bow run up in almost a continuous curve from the bottom, easily deflecting spray and adding buoyancy, while making it an easy boat to run up against a shore or marsh. The earliest garveys (or scows, as they were sometimes known) were cross-planked on the bottom and quite rugged.

There is a contemporary version of this workboat at Graysonville, Maryland, where Tom and Joe Egeberg use plywood and epoxy to produce the Egeberg 16, a strong, high-performance workboat perfect for the shallow waters of the bay. The hull shape has been modified, with sharp V sections leading up to a sort of chicken-breasted bow — wide enough to step on. Like most workboats, the garvey drags a bit at slower speeds, but once up on plane she's steady and stable as a rock. Very modern in performance, solidly built of wood with the right mix of high-tech epoxy, and nicely finished with some traditional touches (such as the mahogany and cherry deck and coamings), the Egeberg garvey represents the continuing evolution of traditional small craft.

CHAPTER SIX

SPORT AND THE MARSHMEN

*F*lashing wings and bright water, cool October mornings on the marshes, and boats that "aren't there." Or at least that is the objective of the duck hunter — to have a capable craft that allows him or her to travel quietly and efficiently over the waters of the flyway as inconspicuously as possible. No fancy brightwork, just a low-sided, lightweight boat, painted a dull drab color and generally covered with reeds or marsh grasses; barely large enough for hunter, decoys, and retriever.

The great American duck boat will, by and large, win no awards for elegance, though some of the shapes are aesthetically appealing. There is no accurate account of the number of designs in use because they vary from region to region, even from one marsh to another. The duck boat is a watercraft with some common requirements but also tailored to the specific nature of a hunting area. Some grounds are in fairly open water, requiring a boat to be seaworthy, while others are in sheltered areas, needing a boat simply to offer a dry, stable place from which to hunt or to wait patiently for a migrating flock of mallards.

The history of the duck boat is not rooted in what is regarded today as a recreational pursuit. In the 1800s waterfowl were a market commodity and the first marshmen were working hunters. Many also were fishermen, and most were skilled, responsible hunters who respected their prey as much as they recognized its economic importance. A few were notorious in their methods, however, and have left a black mark on history. The men who hunted waterfowl for a living were known as market gunners; and the more unsavory of the lot, realizing that at this time waterfowl had not yet

These notorious "market guns" exist today only in museums — grim reminders of the extremes to which some unprincipled hunters once resorted when shooting waterfowl.

learned to be wary of hunters, built crude "market guns" — homemade affairs with several iron pipe barrels mounted on the prows of low skiffs or punts. They would sneak up on a feeding flock and blast away, killing or maiming as many as fifty birds with one shot. The practice was outlawed and although it did not stop immediately, it eventually was brought under control.

The Delaware Ducker

It does not appear as though the duck boat had a specific origin, for in the beginning any small skiff or punt would serve. There were

many small, light boats that were being used on the waterways around the marshes for a variety of purposes — fishing, hunting, and transportation. Eventually, they began to be modified for just waterfowling. The leisure class was well established by the mid-1800s, and one of the boats that proved suitable for ducking appears in a well-known painting by Thomas Eakins, *Will Schuster and Blackman Going Shooting,* painted in 1876. Along the Delaware River at that time, a 15-foot canoelike boat was used for a variety of purposes, both recreational and practical. The boat that was to become known as the Delaware ducker had a very seaworthy hull. Whether it evolved from the whaleboat, canoe, or peapod is not known, but it possessed the same qualities as those craft, especially in open water on the exposed Delaware shore. The ducker was especially well suited for sportsmen: comfortable to row or sail, steady enough to stand in and shoot from, and easily poled through the marshes.

The ducker is built of cedar lapstraked planking formed over a mold. The ribs (about twenty) are then bent into place, fitting into grooves in the gunwale for a tight fit. A short deck is fitted at either end, joined by side decks (washboards) about 4 to 6 inches wide along either side; the cockpit is trimmed with a low, oval coaming that stiffens the hull, adding to the grace of the boat and keeping much of the water out when sailing on an excessive heel. Inside, the bottom is protected by a single removable floorboard. Aft is a removable stern seat, with a triangular platform under the deck to keep extra clothes and lunch dry. Seating amidships is a low, movable box. Oarlocks are mounted on raised sockets so that the boat can be propelled comfortably without hitting the knees with the oars.

For sailing, there are three favored rigs: for gunning in late fall or winter, a simple spritsail is ample; in summer, a larger sprit or gaff is employed; and for racing, a large 100-square-foot gaff or sprit rig provides plenty of action. Since the mast is mounted through the forward deck, there is no provision for a jib, nor is one really needed. The ducker is fitted with a daggerboard, also well forward to be out of the way. The rudder is shaped to fit the curve of the sternpost and has a long, removable tiller.

These boats were actively raced — the

Given the stability of the ducker, poling is an ideal way to explore the marshes quietly.

Philadelphia Yacht Club in 1887 records a course record (for rowing) of three minutes over an hour for a 7-mile run. Under sail the ducker is lively and must be sailed carefully because of its light weight. Yet in a seaway under oars, the boat is as safe as its supposed forebears, the peapod and the whaleboat. Poling along in the marshes, one can stand on the afterdeck without the feeling that the boat might capsize.

Some prime examples of the Delaware ducker survive today — one of the most notable at Mystic Seaport in Mystic, Connecticut. The boat's original owner was John P. York, a bricklayer by trade, who bought her in 1880 and kept her in a boathouse at Bridesburgh, on the Delaware. The Yorks rowed or sailed her downriver to their summer cottage, where she was used for recreation as well as hunting. The boat stayed in the family until York's grandson donated it to Mystic Seaport — in prime condition and fully equipped with all hunting and sailing gear.

As has happened with other notable designs, the ducker is finding a second-generation popularity in reproduction form.

Some have recently been built by boatbuilding schools and private builders for rowing or sailing, perhaps even duck hunting. There is a 21-foot contemporary wooden version being produced in Rhode Island, and a few have been built in fiberglass as well.

When boats such as the ducker are in rare supply, both their origins and exact design details often fall into obscurity. Sometimes a museum or collector may have an example or some bits and pieces of information, but unless an attempt is made to organize, verify, and complete that material, the special qualities of a particular design may become hazy. In the mid-1970s the Apprenticeshop at the Maine Maritime Museum helped organize an effort to build a re-creation of a true 1890s Delaware ducker. The project eventually led to a cooperative effort involving five museums and included interviews with a man who had himself built one based on an original. Such pooling of information and skills is important to maritime preservation and is beginning to be taken seriously, since valuable firsthand knowledge will be impossible to find if it is not documented now.

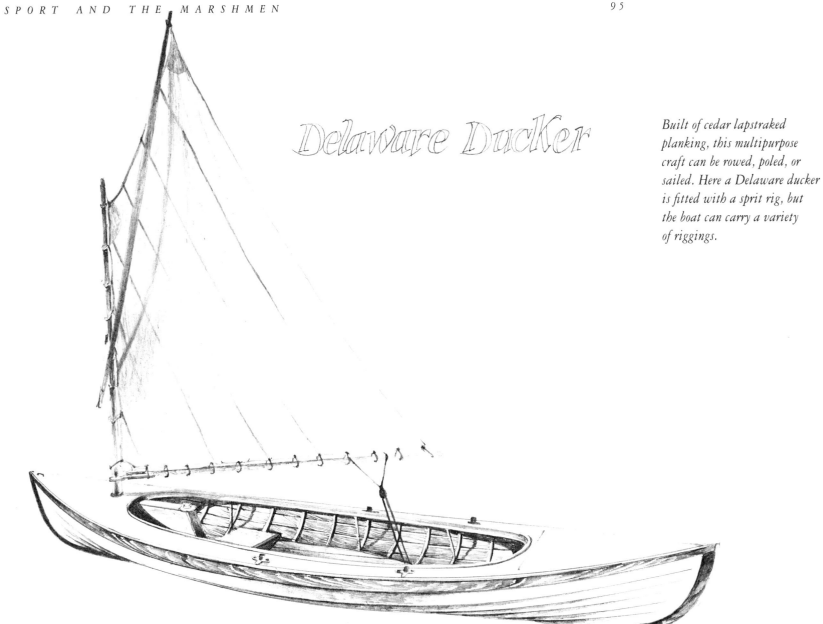

Delaware Ducker

Built of cedar lapstraked planking, this multipurpose craft can be rowed, poled, or sailed. Here a Delaware ducker is fitted with a sprit rig, but the boat can carry a variety of riggings.

The Barnegat Bay Sneak Box

The Barnegat Bay sneak box has a more certain history than the ducker. We know who built the first one and when, but even Hazelton Seaman, its inventor in 1836, probably never envisioned its colorful career.

The sneak box (or "devil's coffin," as it was called when Seaman first built it, for it did indeed resemble one) has a hull and deck that do not seem to be derived from any other boat. It looks almost as though it would work right side up or upside down, save for the cockpit. The bottom is a wide, shallow arc with a spoon bow for both speed and stability, and when pressed under sail, the boat becomes very stiff. What water does rise above the edge has nowhere to go but aft, as the boat is almost all curved deck. The flat transom will just support a rudder or scull. It was designed strictly as a duck-hunting boat and was used by "good guy" market gunners (it was too light for those waterfowl cannons described earlier) until the late nineteenth century. In the beginning it was fitted with a small sprit rig and a centerboard case generally set off-center.

All the elements of this duck boat are there for a reason. The spoon bow made it easy to pull up on a muddy bank. It carried two daggerboards, one about 3 feet long for sailing and the other nearly 7 feet for anchoring the boat in the muddy bottom when hunting. A spray hood was fitted to keep the hunter from the elements, and there was an afterdeck platform to carry decoys. Folding oarlocks would swing out of the way to allow a hunter room to maneuver his gun barrel without rising from the cockpit. There were runners on the bottom for dragging the boat across the ice, and in fact it was discovered that it could even be sailed that way, like an iceboat. The boat is light enough to be rowed, sailed, sculled, poled, or paddled. It can even handle a small outboard motor, and it has overnight or snoozing accommodations for the patient hunter. The sneak box was well designed for its task, and it is still used by some hunters today.

The sneak box received national attention when a well-known small boat adventurer, Nathaniel Bishop, set off from Pittsburgh in his *Centennial Republic* on a 2,600-mile trek down the Ohio and Mississippi rivers to the Gulf of

Mexico and Florida's western shore. Bishop's account, *Four Months in a Sneak Box,* was published in 1879. Aside from being a remarkable experience, the voyage proved the boat's uncanny seaworthiness and handiness under sail.

Yacht and small craft designers such as W.P. Stephens and Henry Rushton (of sailing canoe fame) were soon creating yachtsmen's versions of the hunter's boat. As these became faster and more esoteric, they lost resemblance to duck boats in all but the basic shape, and from the shores of New Jersey's Barnegat Bay and other yacht club playgrounds there appeared a number of racing sneak box fleets.

Today the Barnegat racing fleet has all but vanished — probably superseded by the planing dinghies with their high-tech hardware and the economics of fiberglass production. But Bishop's odyssey presaged the use of sneak boxes for all sorts of transportation (including mail delivery) until 1900. Then the new "super sneaks" began to appear, and with them came formalized racing. The original 12-footer grew to 20 feet, with a gigantic 600 square feet of sail, a crew of six, and some sandbags needed to keep the boat

Though small in size, the sneak box has an efficient layout: the oarlocks fold down, decoys ride on a removable shelf aft, and the sailing rig can be stowed under the deck. Note the long centerboard, which can be pushed down into the muddy bottom of the marsh to anchor the boat in position.

A large crew was needed to handle J.H. Perrine's Adagio, *when under racing rig.*

upright. This was regarded as much as derring-do as sport, and the giants soon gave way to a more prudent, though still fast, 15-footer designed by J.H. Perrine in 1918. So successful was this boat that it remained the dominant racing class of all sailboats on the Barnegat until the late 1950s, by which time Perrine's shop had turned out nearly three thousand. Other builders were successful in their shops as well and offered a variety of rigs from gaff cat to Marconi sloop. A few slightly larger sizes sometimes were built, though none was so unwieldy as the first racer of 1900.

Craftsmanship of the Perrine boats was of the highest order and may have contributed to their decline as well, since by the time of Perrine's death, cheaper plywood, hard-chined boats were common and there wasn't time or money to build the carefully constructed sneak boxes. A few were tried in fiberglass, but this did not work because fiberglass is noisy and thus not good for sneaking up on ducks.

The Barnegat Bay sneak box still has its attraction: It's one of those designs that, like the Beetle cat, is stable and forgiving. Some plans have been modified for home builders to use

with plywood, and a few shops will build a
custom sneak box on special order. Very few of
Perrine's boats are left, but one, appropriately
named *Adagio,* has been restored and is still
sailing. In 1985 a modern-day adventurer,
Christopher Cunningham, built a high-tech
version of Nathaniel Bishop's sneak box and
repeated Bishop's odyssey down the Mississippi
River to Florida — the ultimate compliment to a
tiny boat.

*   *   *

From the sublime to the simple, from
sneak box to sink box. The sink box just barely
fits the definition of a watercraft, yet it fulfills
the needs of the hunter — to be as close to the
mark as possible without being seen. In spite of
its name the sink box is meant to float; it is a
square box with a wide platform all around it to
keep it from sinking. A stationary boat
incapable of moving on its own, it can't be
rowed, paddled, powered, or sailed. Yet
thousands of them have been built. Towed to a
favorite spot, anchored for possibly the season, it
could best be described as a floating duck blind.

Some duck boats are just a step above that —
movable. While there are innumerable
variations on the theme, the following are
representative of the many types of duck boats
working the Atlantic flyway.

*Given its inability to move on its
own, the sink box is a boat only
when it is being towed to a
favorite hunting spot.*

The Merrymeeting Bay Sneak Boats

Five great rivers, led by the Kennebec, enter the huge freshwater marshland known as Merrymeeting Bay in midcoast Maine. Here thousands of acres of wild rice create a natural habitat to feed millions of ducks and geese that migrate along the East Coast. In the middle of

the bay sits Swan Island, which was the traditional meeting place of the Indian tribes of Maine – the Penobscot, Passamaquoddy, Kennebec, and Micmac. Here in the summer the Indians harvested thousands of waterfowl and smoked their meat for the vital winter food supply. This was also where a successful decoy trade developed, with local makers such as John Trefethen and Sam Toothacher. Being a prime waterfowl hunting area, this wide, extensive marshland fostered the development of the Merrymeeting boat.

The Merrymeeting boat is of the most utilitarian sort: short, nearly flat bottomed, with a wide foredeck and high coamings. A hole in the transom would allow a gunner to scull the boat while lying down, with just his head visible as he worked his way forward. Some of the Merrymeeting boats had pointed bows, while others were blunt. Along the side and fore decks would be stringers or slats under which marsh grass could be secured to disguise the portable duck blind when the boat reached its destination.

Merrymeeting Bay is wide and convoluted with many choice but hidden areas, as well as

Two basic Merrymeeting Bay sneak boats. Although usually rowed, they can accommodate a small outboard motor, which is a welcome addition in Maine's vast hunting areas.

The Great South Bay scooter, a variation on the South Bay duck boat, could reach 40 to 50 miles an hour on the ice.

tricky tidal currents. Consequently, a substantial guide trade developed here. Although its heyday was around 1890, guide service is still available today.

The Great South Bay Duck Boat

Great South Bay on Long Island is an exposed expanse of shallow, often choppy water. A suitable duck boat for this area had to do more than sneak up on ducks – it had to be able to maneuver well in the shallow water and strong winds of the bay. Being close to New York City, Great South Bay supported a substantial market-gunning business, and as winter was the favored season, any boat here would have to be capable of handling patches of ice at times. Captain Wilbur Corwin designed a ducker that was similar to the Barnegat but had nearly rounded ends and two runners set about 16 inches apart on the bottom for ice sailing. It was a very buoyant boat, quite capable in foul weather, and it too found itself being raced.

The New Hampshire Duck Boat

In the marshes of New Hampshire along the Merrimack River, there exists a duck boat that no one would ever try to adapt to any other purpose. It looks like one half of a very long kayak. It has a narrow V shape and is 17 feet long and barely 4 feet wide at the extreme stern. The cockpit is only in the after third of the boat; the rest is all "snout" to ride over the choppy waves of the marshes. Inside the prow is a lead weight to keep the bow down in heavy weather. Fastened to a pulley, the weight can be pulled back to the cockpit for better balance on calm days. Rowing, sculling, and a very small outboard motor are the only propulsion options; sailing is out of the question. This is a very successful design for one man and a dog, and though its origins are obscure, it is still occasionally seen in the area.

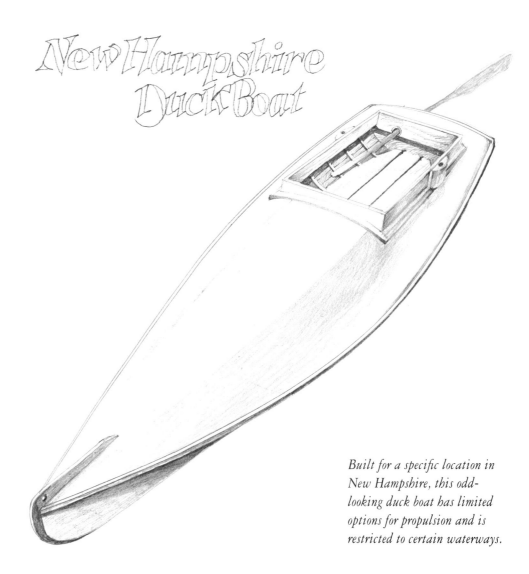

New Hampshire Duck Boat

Built for a specific location in New Hampshire, this odd-looking duck boat has limited options for propulsion and is restricted to certain waterways.

*A Chesapeake decoy
carver working in his shop
in the off-season.*

*   *   *

This is just a sample of the range of duck boat styles. Except perhaps for the Delaware ducker and the Barnegat Bay sneak box, none has ever been mass-produced, as they are generally home built according to the waterfowler's taste and experience. You can buy a generic sneak box through the undisputed bible of sporting equipment — L.L. Bean's Hunting and Fishing Catalog. Or if you have ever kicked around a Sears outlet, you may have noticed the aluminum skiffs painted either olive drab or camouflage — today's more readily available version of the duck boat, though a good deal less romantic in history and of doubtful "sneakability."

CHAPTER SEVEN

FLAT-WATER SAILING

By the mid-1800s the population along the East Coast had grown to such an extent that there was an increasing demand for fish and seafood. A wide variety and large quantity existed, but harvesting often had to be done in shallow bays and rivers. Just as the waters of the Chesapeake required special craft, so did those of New England and Florida, where the catboat and sharpie-type fishing boats developed.

The Sharpie

We can only speculate as to the origins of certain boats, but this is not the case with the sharpie. The sharpie exists because it satisfied a need in the most direct manner possible. It is probably the most boat for the least expense, the easiest to build, and the most uncomplicated to rig and sail. In essence, the sharpie is a long skiff with sails. Considering the fact that it was first built simply to do a job, it could have been forgiven if it turned out ugly. Except for a few that were poorly constructed, however, form followed function in such a sublime manner that its striking beauty was almost inevitable.

Howard Chapelle in his *American Small Sailing Craft* begins his discussion of the sharpie with the introduction of the flatiron skiff, and with good reason. The latter's construction, based on a cross-planked bottom, is what made the longer sharpie's form possible. Though later adapted for sail, the skiff's first prerequisites were that it row well, have a flat bottom for easy beaching, and be of simple, light construction. Simple straight boards could be nailed across the bottom, giving it enough strength to eliminate the need for a heavy frame; the sides required only a few light ribs to align the planking. Since

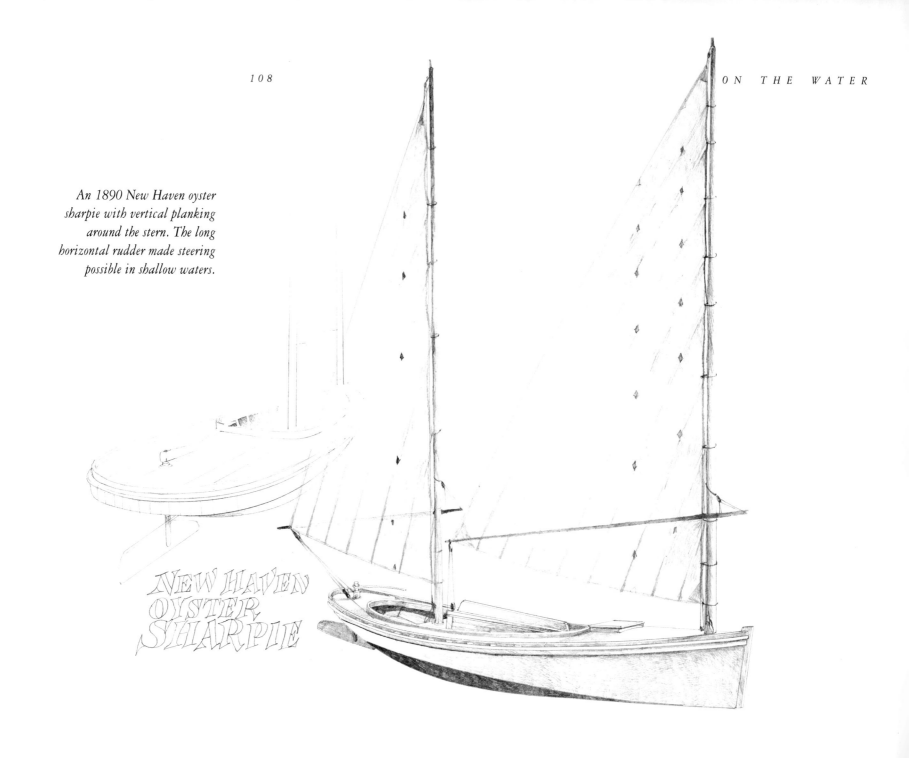

An 1890 New Haven oyster
sharpie with vertical planking
around the stern. The long
horizontal rudder made steering
possible in shallow waters.

NEW HAVEN
OYSTER
SHARPIE

all surfaces were flat, and the sides slightly flared, there was hardly any need for complicated lofting or curving of planks.

The first skiffs had a bottom that was flat from bow to stern, but this caused so much drag aft that gradually the bottom was curved up to the waterline. This made the boat quicker and easier to row without sacrificing much of its load-carrying ability. When a larger skiff was built to accommodate sailing rigs for the oyster trade around New Haven, Connecticut, the elevated stern made the skiff a fast and easily tacked sailboat.

A sharpie is generally regarded as being a flat-bottomed boat with flared sides, a straight stem, two masts, and a bottom beam-to-length ratio of about 1 to 4 or 6. It is a fairly long, narrow boat, but it has good stability because of its hard, low chines and flared sides. It probably first appeared in New England but is known south to Florida and west to the Great Lakes. It has undergone a wide variety of traditional and contemporary interpretations, most of which pay tribute to its simplicity and grace.

It is believed that the first sharpies to appear in any number were built around New Haven after the oyster beds that could be reached by rowing had begun to be depleted. By 1870 the New Haven sharpies were well established and were of two types: boats between 20 and 30 feet, which were primarily operated by one man, since the profit in smaller catches often did not allow the luxury of a paid hand; and two- or three-man boats between 30 and 65 feet. The smaller boats were characterized by having three mast steps; in poor weather the aftermast could be unshipped and the foremast stepped a ways back from the bow, making the boat easier for one person to handle.

Everything on a sharpie seems to have developed for a purpose. At first the boats had the square stern of the skiff, but as the tongers often worked from the stern, they soon rounded off the corners and made it a continuous curve so the tongs would not hang up on the corners. To keep construction simple, instead of steam-bending planks around the stern, an internal framework was made and covered with short, vertical boards. There was no skeg aft because it would inhibit tacking, but a substantial rudder was needed to turn such a long boat. The rudder could not, however, be so deep as to drag on the bottom of the oyster shallows. The solution was a long (up to 6-foot) rudder that was shallow and balanced. About a third of it was forward of the rudder post, and it was mounted so it could be pushed down in deeper water or raised for the shallows.

The longer sharpies of the mid- to late nineteenth century were cross-planked on the bottom, but their greater length needed stiffening, so three boards were placed on edge, cut to the curve of the bottom and run most of the length of the hull, except for the extreme ends. One board was left out where the centerboard would go, and this made a strong base for the centerboard trunk. There was a point, however, where practicality nearly defeated itself. Since the early sharpies were used primarily for oystering, they needed as much open boat as possible to hold the catch. The place where the masts were positioned was stiffened by seats across the boat, but in the case of the aftermast, the seats got in the way. So the mast was fastened to the after end of the centerboard case. With this arrangement, however, a strong wind would work the mast and cause the boat to weaken and leak. To remedy this problem, a temporary thwart would be placed across the centerboard.

The sharpie rig is a marvel of sailing efficiency. The masts, which are freestanding, are fairly thick at the bottom but taper to just a couple of inches at the top, which makes them quite flexible. Traditional sharpie sails have no booms at the lower edge, thus eliminating the danger of a crewman being hit on the head by a swinging boom. In addition, the sprit is fastened several feet above the clew, and this arrangement keeps the sail down when going before the wind and reduces the potential for capsizing in an unintentional jibe. Reefing, or shortening the sail, is a little more difficult, but sometimes this is done by turning the masts and rolling up the sails a little way around them. There is greater sailing efficiency with free-turning masts as well, since the flow of air around the mast can be more direct. The whole rig is essentially self-tending: There is no jib to have to bring around on each tack, and since the masts can be taken down (albeit by a very strong and agile crew), the sharpie's narrow bottom and raised stern sections allow it to be rowed or poled efficiently in calm waters.

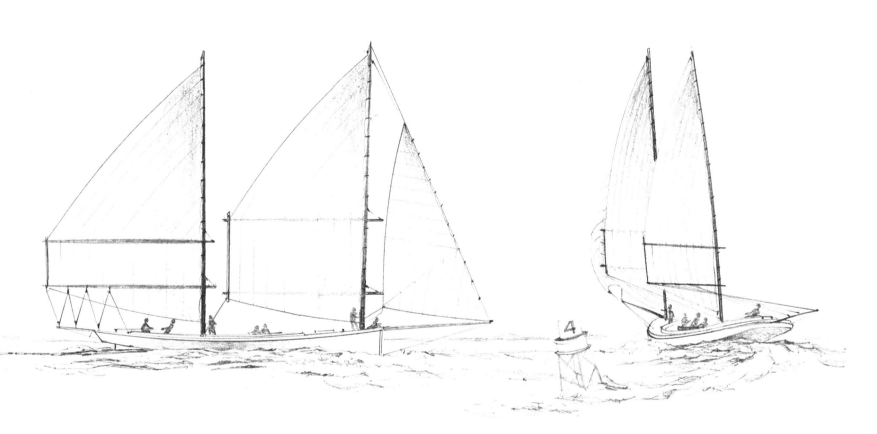

Yachtsmen along the Connecticut shore soon noticed that this "sailing pickup truck" was as fast as it was graceful, and by 1870 specially designed racing sharpies began to appear at the summer club races. Construction was basically the same as for the workboats, except for a flatter run aft and a little more beam to handle the increased sail area that every racer is wont to crowd on his boat. Black walnut bulkheads, varnished coamings, and slick paint jobs on the racers made it easy to tell from a distance whether the sharpie was for working or

Working sharpies needed to be first to market with their catch and thus were swift sailers. Yachtsmen recognized their potential and fine-tuned them to be first across the finish line.

racing, although the absence of the ever-present flock of gulls that follows every fishing boat also made this obvious. By the 1880s the rigs distinguished racers even more, with bowsprits and stern outriggers, huge sails with double sprits, and a sort of square sail-spinnaker for downwind speed. As with racing canoes, it took a half ton of live crew on springboards to hold a racing sharpie level, but this made for exciting spectator sport on a Sunday afternoon. Speed records were set that some slick fiberglass sloops of today would envy, in one case averaging 16 knots for three consecutive hours.

In 1875 a North Carolina oysterman saw the New Haven sharpies and had a noted Connecticut builder, Charles Graves, build and deliver one to his home port of Beaufort. It not only outsailed local boats, but it proved itself so capable in the fierce gales that sweep the North Carolina coast that it soon replaced them. The Carolina sharpie was a bit broader in the stern and was generally about 45 feet long, usually fitted with a small cabin well forward, as the Carolina fishermen tended to go far afield.

Florida has always held a fascination for northerners, and probably even more so for those who enjoy being on the water. Ralph Munroe was a Staten Islander who in 1877 migrated south to Biscayne Bay in Florida. An experienced sailor and acquaintance of Nathaniel Herreshoff, a widely known Rhode Island boat designer and builder, he had a sharpie built up north and shipped to his new sailing grounds, thereby introducing the type to local waters. Munroe became the first postmaster of Coconut Grove and delivered the mail by boat — in a 30-foot New Haven sharpie that surprised the native conch fishermen by beating them to windward.

Munroe's fascination with the design led to many variations on the theme, including a 41-foot Presto ketch with "soft" chines, designed for shoal-draft (shallow-water) cruising. A series of Presto types was built, but by 1885 Munroe decided he needed to go back to a more utilitarian boat — one that could sail out in Biscayne Bay to meet incoming ships for the mail and supplies he would then take to the settlers at Lake Worth, 70 miles inland. *Egret* was a 28-foot hard-chined sharpie — lightly built but strong, fast, and seaworthy — which could carry an amazing amount of freight and mail.

Munroe's original *Egret* is lost, except for one or two faded photographs, but the knowledge of her unique qualities has inspired the building of others.

The sharpie may have originated in New England, where it served its working purpose well, but in its second life it seems tailor-made for the shallows of the Florida Keys. Billy Schwicker is a modern-day Florida adventurer who has both promoted the sharpie in print and spent most of his free time taking advantage of the boat's simplicity and shoal-water capability. Because he is a free spirit who strives to make his own life as unencumbered as possible, it was natural for him to be attracted to Ralph Munroe's *Egret*. An experienced sailor, Bill has worked for the Outward Bound school in Big Pine Key, Florida, and believes in the self-reliant attitude promoted by the school. He did research on the *Egret,* sought sound advice from experts, and then built his own plywood version of it. Although the materials changed, the concept of utilitarian building methods did not, and thus the twentieth-century *Egret* remains faithful to the soul of the original.

Schwicker's boat was an interpretation, so

Bill Schwicker with his 28-foot adaptation of Ralph Munroe's sharpie *Egret.*

Built with the same materials and methods, Robert Jones's Grimalken *is an exact replica of the* Egret.

he was able to build it inexpensively. Robert Jones, however, wanted to build a replica of the *Egret* with the same materials and methods as the original. He collaborated with Graham Ero of the Sound School of Boatbuilding in New Haven, Connecticut, and although their boat, *Grimalken,* is handsome and inspiring, it cost about thirty times what the original did.

The sharpie has appeared as a type in more places than any other boat in the country. It was known on Lake Champlain in Vermont as a pleasure boat; schooner sharpies were used in the halibut fisheries in the Strait of Juan de Fuca north of Seattle, Washington; and square-sterned fishing sharpies were commonly seen on the Great Lakes. Almost every combination of masts and sails has been tried on these boats, but for the most part the cat or ketch rig seems to be the best. The sharpie still remains the best boat for the least money, at least for shoal-draft cruising, and in its simplicity, it is one of the most beautiful.

The Catboat

Catboats are round-bilged, heavily built planked boats, and in contrast to the sharpies, they are not easily made. There is an extreme ratio of length to width — usually two to one. They are deepest aft, with a long, straight keel to which is attached the "barn door" rudder, usually one-sixth the length of the waterline, needed to counter the huge sail that often extends several feet beyond the stern. The sheer is low aft to allow working over the sides, but it is quite high at the bow to keep breaking waves from swamping the boat. A small cuddy is placed well forward, allowing a large and deep working cockpit. Construction is generally of pine or cedar planking over heavy, closely spaced frames to give the boat strength and durability, which is essential. The single mast is unstayed and rather massive (the foot often being 12 inches across) and exerts an enormous strain on the hull.

I wouldn't go so far as to say I've never seen an ugly boat, but virtually all types have their own special grace and appeal. The sharpie is handsome because of its simplicity and lithe nature; the catboat is appealing because of its often graceful shape despite its massive construction. There have been some

Designed purely as a recreational craft, the Great South Bay catboat was both graceful and fast.

contemporary hard-chined catboats developed for easier amateur building, but the classical cats seem to draw their style from a careful shaping of curves and coamings to unify the rather short, blunt hull shape. Some of the later racing and yacht types approach sheer elegance — a credit to the persistence of the designers.

As soon as engines became suitable for saltwater conditions (around 1910), they were added to working catboats. The hull of the boat is deep aft of the centerboard, allowing room to install power below the cockpit floor. The safety advantage is as important as it is convenient, since Cape Cod and Buzzards Bay can be frustratingly calm in summer and treacherous in a blow. Often catboats worked in winter strictly as powerboats, the rig being left ashore. Unlike some sailing craft, the catboat adapted to power without much modification of hull, for the broad aft section easily supported the extra thrust without making the boat "squat" in the water.

By the 1880s, with the summer trade in flower in catboat territory, racing and party cats soon appeared. Escaping the heat of the cities, the leisure class was attracted to the long, sandy

Sails at the turn of the century were made of heavy cotton and would quickly mildew if furled while wet. Consequently, drying sail was a common sight in harbors, such as this one in Nantucket.

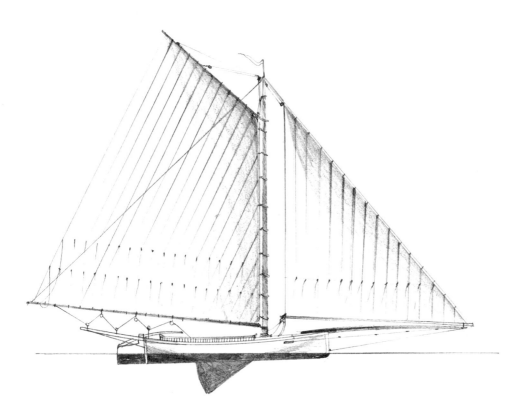

The sandbagger Annie *shows the huge amount of sail that such a racing craft could carry.*

sound. Soon special party boats were built with more finish and even tufted velvet seats.

The Great South Bay catboat was designed and built by Gilbert Smith on Long Island in 1890. It had a slack bilge and a very low, graceful sheer. Although used often as a party boat, it was fast and frequently raced. An unrestored example of this boat can be seen at Mystic Seaport in Mystic, Connecticut, as can another, in full working order, of the most extreme racing form – the sandbagger *Annie*. This boat is properly termed a cat-sloop, and although built at a time when catboats were still used for fishing, the resemblance is slight. *Annie* has the beam of the cat but almost nothing underwater, and though the hull is 28 feet long, her bowsprit and boomkin extend the overall length to twice that. The boom is so long that in order to reef it, an intrepid crew member had to crawl out along it – not the most reassuring place to be, especially if there was an unintentional jibe. The eight-member crew hung over the side to try to keep the boat upright, and bags of sand were carried in the cockpit to be shifted from side to side after each tack. Thus the name sandbagger. Fast they were, and

beaches of Cape Cod, Nantucket, Martha's Vineyard, and Long Island Sound, as well as the Jersey Shore. On Nantucket, long a posh summer resort, the huge interiors of the working cats were sometimes cleaned up to take as many as twenty or thirty people on outings around the

A fleet of catboats racing on Nantucket Sound. With the wind just a little behind the beam, catboats exhibit their best sailing characteristics, making a good 7 knots with ease and sailing as steady as a train on a set of tracks.

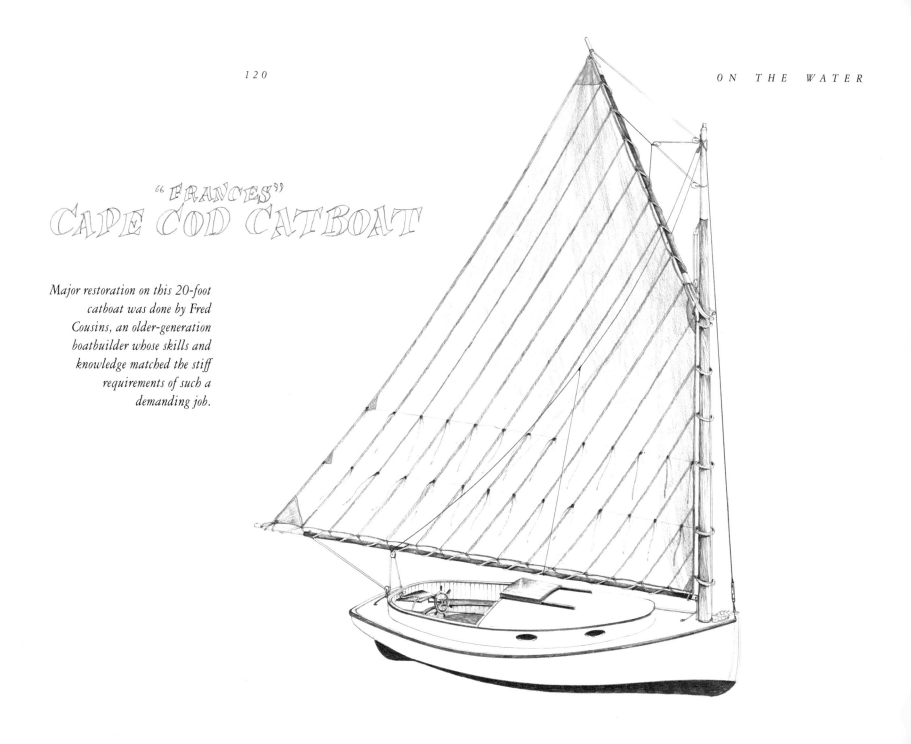

"FRANCES"
CAPE COD CATBOAT

Major restoration on this 20-foot catboat was done by Fred Cousins, an older-generation boatbuilder whose skills and knowledge matched the stiff requirements of such a demanding job.

capsize they did. One speculates that much as the spectators along the Mystic River enjoyed the races, they also anticipated the spills as often as the crowd at Indianapolis today expects to see a race car spin out at 150 miles an hour.

On Cape Cod the name Crosby is synonymous with catboats. At Osterville, in one of the tuckaway harbors of the Cape's south shore, Wilton Crosby started a boatyard in the late 1880s that over a fifty-year span turned out some of the most finely crafted and attractive catboats. The Crosby yard is still there, and though no longer actively building catboats, it does have an interest in preservation and restoration. In 1969 the seventy-two-year-old Crosby cruising catboat *Frances* was donated to Mystic Seaport, and a major restoration was undertaken there ten years later. Restoration demands patience and affection: Badly deteriorated parts must be replicated by careful measuring and in some cases estimating; rotted frames must be replaced a few at a time so the hull won't lose its shape; and since early boats were iron fastened, not only are the nails and screws rusted out, but new bronze screws cannot be put back in the same positions. Special tools

often must be devised, since moldings available then are now extinct. Sometimes the skills or techniques of a particular era are obscure, making precise restoration difficult. Fortunately for Mystic Seaport, Fred Cousins, an older-generation boatbuilder, was able to restore the 20-foot *Frances,* which is on permanent display at the museum.

After about 1920 the catboat fell out of favor with fishermen, and it was not until 1962 that Breck Marshall pioneered the use of fiberglass to bring back a boat that was now almost impossible to reproduce in wood. Today about a dozen small companies make catboats, from a small fiberglass version of the Beetle cat (see Chapter Eight) to large 26-footers. Designers such as Charles Wittholz and Frederick Groeller also have produced plans for many small and attractive catboats for amateur building.

The catboat is fortunate in having an active association similar to the Friendship Sloop Society. Its members are interested in racing, preserving original boats, and promoting the catboat through medium-class meets of modern fiberglass boats.

CHAPTER EIGHT

THE
BOATS
OF
SUMMER

*T*he pure joy of a summer afternoon's sail is perfectly expressed in Winslow Homer's painting *Breezing Up*. Though the helm in the picture is under the control of a grown-up, several boys with their own dreams in their heads are enjoying the outing. A lot of us went sailing for the first time like that, later setting out in boats of our own. Perhaps it was a skiff or a punt with a bamboo mast and an old sheet for a sail; or maybe, if we had a generous parent, something a little more exotic.

The boats of our youth were vehicles for our imaginations – fantasies with wooden edges – and teachers of real life at the same time. Sometimes if the fever were high, we even built our own craft, though it's a wonder some of us ever went to sea again after a first experiment with naval architecture. Nevertheless, whether in a square-toed punt or fast little daysailer, the fresh excitement of being on the water by yourself has to be a high point of growing up.

Most of us envision eighteenth-century America as being too hard at work to enjoy the pleasures of boats. But just as fishermen would engage in a bit of racing "just on the way home, you know," young people also would set out on grand adventures down the bay anytime they could get their hands on the family skiff. Once in a while an indulgent father would build his children a small version of a working craft; it was a good way to introduce them to the ways of the sea, from which most would eventually earn their living. Boys went to work early in the 1700s, and many were quite capable seamen before they could shave; thus a little competitive boating has probably been in every waterman's blood.

By the late 1800s a large leisure class had

Since 1887, the North Haven dinghy has been a popular boat, both for racing and for purely pleasure sailing.

taken to the seaside. In 1887 the first recognized one-design sailing dinghy was being built on the island of North Haven in Maine. Derived, no doubt, from a fishing boat, this 14-foot cat-rigged sailboat became so popular that it has been built and raced for the past hundred years. (One-design boats are controlled by an association so that hull form, weight, sail area, and allowed equipment are the same for every boat in the fleet — thus ensuring that each competitor has an even chance and must depend on his racing skill to win.)

The North Haven dinghy is built of carvel planking over bent oak ribs and has much the same stability as its relative the peapod. But its fine, sharp bow and lighter construction, combined with its large gaff sail, make it a quick and lively sailer. It is often built as a reproduction boat today by boatbuilding schools and also has been made of fiberglass, carefully designed to keep it within the racing rules.

With the advent of the North Haven boat and other one-design sailing dinghies, an era of purely recreational boatbuilding had begun. Other rowing and sailing craft had developed in isolated instances long before this time, however,

for a few "gentlemen's boats" are recorded in England as early as the fifteenth century. Yachting as a sport dates from around 1800, and the first *America*'s Cup race took place in New York in 1870. The *America,* though derived from a working pilot schooner, was a sleek and fast yacht, and it is not surprising that men of leisure would begin to adapt "modern" design to small craft.

By 1900 custom-built racing yachts were flourishing. The well-known designers of the day did not ignore the needs of young sailors, however, and nearly every large yacht yard turned out its share of daysailers and tenders. Nathaniel Herreshoff, a widely respected New England boat designer and builder, was himself enamored of small boats and designed a wide range of rowing and sailing types. The earliest were variations on yacht tenders but quickly became quite sophisticated.

Probably none is more famous or enduring than the Buzzards Bay 12½, designed in 1914 and built in one form or another ever since that time. The Herreshoff yard made three hundred sixty 12½s from 1914 to 1943. After the war, the Quincy Adams yard built around fifty, then

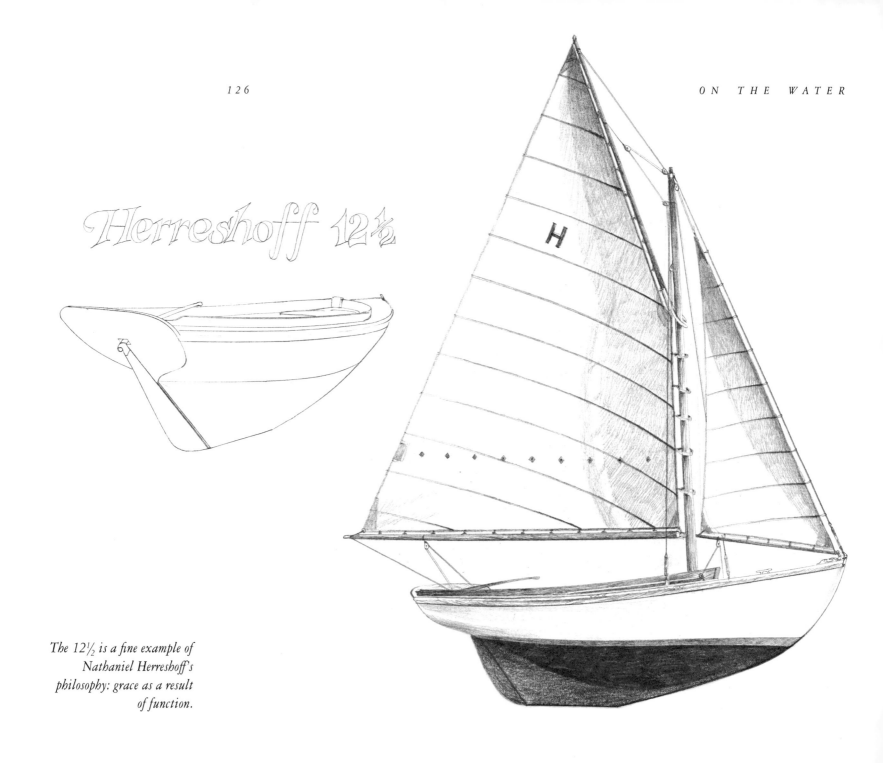

Herreshoff 12½

The 12½ is a fine example of Nathaniel Herreshoff's philosophy: grace as a result of function.

sold the rights to Cape Cod Shipbuilding, which built thirty more wooden ones before switching to fiberglass in the 1950s. Since then the slightly modified design, now called a Bullseye, has remained popular, with more than eight hundred having been built. In recent years traditional wooden replicas and fiberglass versions have been produced. This means that a large number of people have enjoyed the fine qualities of this summer boat for more than half a century.

The 12½ is not a beach boat; it is heavy by design and has a full keel. The boat is actually 15 feet 10 inches in length; 12½ refers to the boat's waterline length. It is one of Nathaniel Herreshoff's best small craft designs. With its gaff mainsail and small jib, it is well balanced, fast, and capable of handling the often rough waters of Buzzards Bay, where it was most likely to be sailed. The boats were originally built upside down over molds on the boat shop floor and conformed to Herreshoff's strict rules of quality yacht construction — so much so that many originals are still sailing.

The 12½, with its varnished transom, coamings, and spars, and its elegant appearance, has never been an inexpensive boat, and being a heavy displacement "small yacht," it is not easily launched from a trailer. After the Great Depression, the Herreshoff Manufacturing Company turned most of its production efforts toward more affordable boats, such as the Amphi-Craft. Developed by Herreshoff's oldest son, Sydney, in 1936, this 13-footer could be rowed, sailed, or fitted with an outboard motor, and it came with a custom trailer. It was further reputed to be "ideal for hunting, fishing, camping and picnicking," reflecting the changing times and hardly descriptive of a yachtsman's lifestyle. But it was still a Herreshoff, well built and well designed, although in its attempt to suit a wide variety of needs, it was probably not too exciting as a racer. The Herreshoff yard at Bristol, Rhode Island, no longer builds boats, but it has recently been reopened as a museum by Halsey Herreshoff, Nathaniel's grandson. It is a fascinating place to visit and exhibits some of the artifacts from yachting's grand era.

Many other dinghy-class boats were designed and built in the period from 1900 to the 1960s. Among them were the Snipe, the

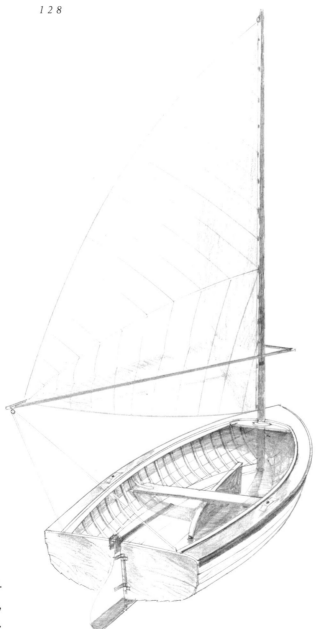

The Amphi-Craft — an all-purpose dinghy for rowing, sailing, or power boating.

Thistle, and probably one of the best-known boats in America, the Sunfish. Two larger recreational racers from the same era are worth mentioning because of their influence on modern one-design sailing. Though hardly "boys' boats," the International Star and the Lightning have been two of the most widely enjoyed and raced small boats in this country.

The Star was designed by Francis Sweisguth in 1911, and except for rig changes and eventually fiberglass hulls, its concept has remained unchanged since that time. Rather than produce it in only one yard, the designers licensed builders so that it would receive wider distribution throughout the country. Consequently, more than five hundred different yards have built this craft. The Star is a hard-chined boat, 22 feet 8 inches in length and 5 feet 8 inches (narrow) in beam. It has a fixed keel with a depth of 3 feet 4 inches, ballasted with 830 pounds of iron. Obviously a deep-water boat, it marked the beginning of national competitions and was one of the first boats to be officially raced in the Olympic Games.

The Lightning-class sloop has served as a family boat as well as an all-out racer. In 1938 a

group of ardent racers on Skaneateles Lake in New York State were looking for a lively, shallow-draft boat that would combine speed with daysailing comfort. They commissioned Olin Stephens, one of the most successful designers of ocean racing boats, to come up with such a craft, and he did. Called the Lightning,

Stars of today, with their refined hulls and sophisticated spars, sails, and hardware, remain popular and competitive racers.

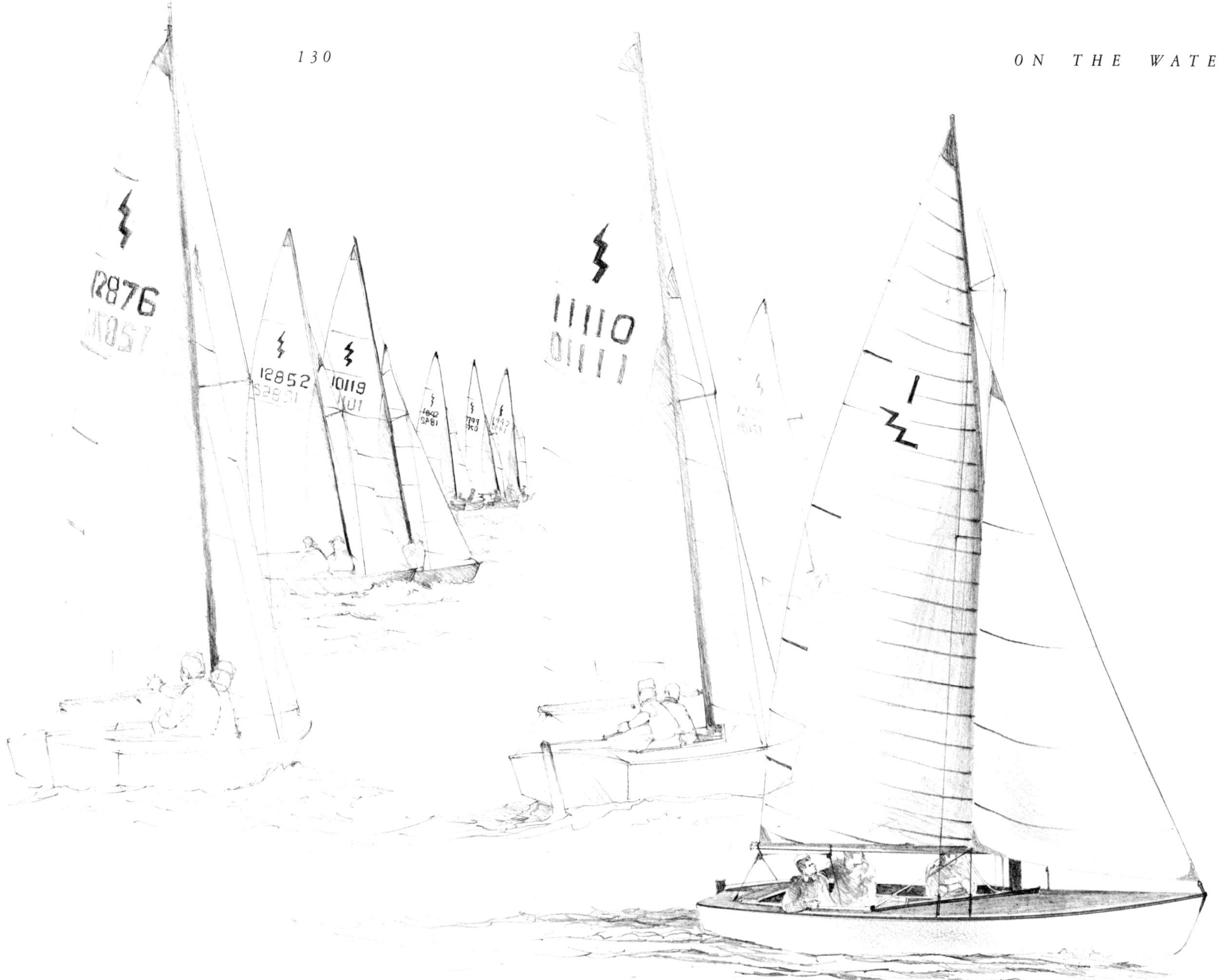
12876
12852
10119
11110

this new sloop was so capable that an account of Stephens's sailing the boat in its first sea trials describes him as removing the tiller while sailing close-hauled in a 25-knot breeze to demonstrate her balance and stability. At 19 feet, the Lightning weighs only 700 pounds, less than the ballast of the Star, yet she has proven herself to be one of the best all-around boats in the country. Though there are fiberglass versions in production today, many of the old cedar and mahogany ones are still competitive, prompting a recent move to redesign the construction for epoxy and plywood building.

The emergence of these fast racing sloops by no means meant the end of more conventional, if slower, recreational watercraft. One classic from the 1920s is the Cape Cod Beetle cat, a descendant of working catboats, not yachtsmen's commissions.

The Beetle family of Clark's Point, New Bedford, Massachusetts, had been boatbuilders for generations. Their primary product was the Beetle whaleboat, known far and wide as the best in the trade and used for a purpose that no seaman who ever practiced whaling would call recreational. These light cedar whaleboats of around 30 feet were lowered over the sides of whaleships to pursue the then plentiful gray whale. When harpooned, a whale would take the crew on what was known as a "Nantucket sleigh ride" — often lasting for hours until the whale tired enough to be brought alongside the mother ship. Sometimes the whale won, either capsizing the whaleboat or breaking it in half. Nonetheless, the Beetle whaleboats were very strong for their size and extremely seaworthy.

After the whaling trade fell off, the Beetle shop turned to smaller boats, including the 25- to 30-foot working catboats needed around Cape Cod. The Beetle family were ingenious in their building methods and in one day could plank up a boat built over a form, with the ribs put in later. This made them competitive, and with the reputation they had earned for quality, the shop prospered long after the whaling trade declined. When in 1920 they began building recreational catboats, they turned their experience to advantage and made the Beetle cat affordable for nearly anyone.

The boat itself was first designed for one of the younger members of the family, but it proved to be so popular that soon John Beetle

Facing page: A montage of Lightnings. These lively, shallow-draft sloops combine speed with daysailing comfort.

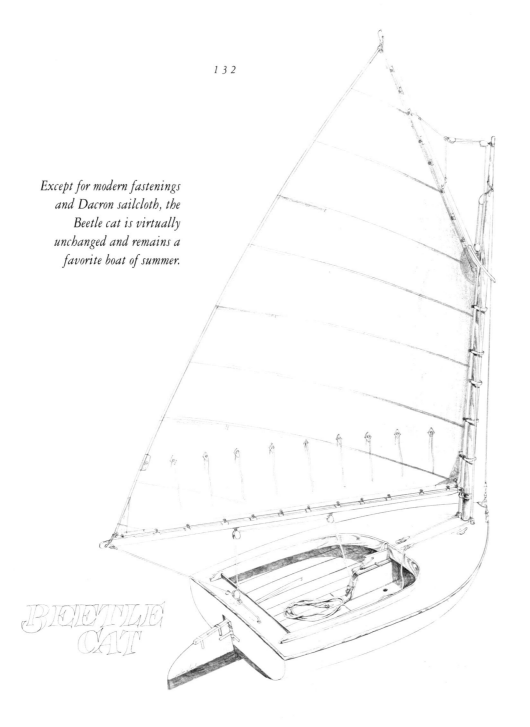

Except for modern fastenings and Dacron sailcloth, the Beetle cat is virtually unchanged and remains a favorite boat of summer.

began full-time production of the tiny catboat. Upon his death in 1928, his daughter, Ruth Beetle, took over management of the company. In addition to being a schoolteacher, Miss Beetle was the only woman shipwright in the country at the time.

World War II ended the full-time production of the Beetle cat, and after the war only a few wooden ones were built by Ruth's brother Carl before he sold production rights to a fiberglass builder. Later he transferred all rights, molds, and title to the wooden design to the Concordia Company of South Dartmouth, Massachusetts. Its then owner Waldo Howland had owned a Beetle cat and had a special fondness for the design. He too was descended from whaleboat builders and had a personal understanding of the virtues of this craft.

By 1948 the Beetle cat had proved to be such a success that the New England Beetle Cat Association was formed. The association's handbook gives a fine description of the boat's special qualities:

> The Beetle Cat Boat is rich in history that stems from whaling days. But what are the features that have given it such wide

acceptance? The wide beam, with the rudder not extending below the bottom of the keel, and centerboard that lifts up are features that lend this boat to shallow waters. It is a boat that can be beached. The great beam (6') makes it unusually stable and gives it a large carrying capacity. While racing standards call for a skipper and one person as crew, these boats have been known to carry as many as six 150 lb. persons. Made entirely of wood (oak frame, cedar planking) with no ballast, it is unsinkable. The large decked area forward on the boat means spray falls on the deck rather than inside the boat. The rig is similar to that used on the old, large-sized Cape Cod catboats, with the mast well forward and using a single sail. With this type of rig, if you release the tiller the boat will head into the wind and practically stop. This feature makes it an ideal boat for youngsters. There is a great deal to be said for a gaff rig on a catboat — you can shorten sail and keep the center of effort where you want it without fear of the boat taking charge and falling off. The bow of the boat is generous in proportion, so that even a large man can stand on it without tipping over — a feature that is much appreciated when landing at a dock or float. The Beetle Cat is a perfect type of boat for learning the fundamentals of sailing because of its safety features.

A Visit to the Beetle Cat Shop

The appearance of boat shops, with rare exceptions, seems to belie the handsome, carefully crafted products that emerge from their doors. Each tends to be a rambling, elderly barn of a place, not a foot longer or wider than is needed, and cluttered with old boats, lumber, and reminders of the past. The tools are nearly always the same — an old but well-made bandsaw, a planer, a drill press, a table saw of indeterminate age, an equally ancient steam box for bending frames, and cluttered benches filled with well-used, well-sharpened if not fancy hand tools. And in the case of the Beetle cat shop, there is a mold that, while still very usable and true, shows the marks of age, since it has been used for every Beetle cat built since 1960.

A successful wooden-boat shop invariably contains at least one other asset — its master builder. Leo J. Telesmanick has been "Mr. Beetle cat" since 1964, though he apprenticed long before that time. Now officially retired, Leo still works in the shop a few days a week for part of the year, the rest being devoted to fishing. The new crew is young, but all have learned the

patient and careful skills at the hands of the master. They build about fifty boats a year now, and there seems to be no end to the customer waiting list. Today's Beetle cat is virtually unchanged from the first, save for bronze fastenings and Dacron sails.

The boats are built along one side of a large building that also serves as the winter resting place for others. Some of these boats are there for freshening up, others for a complete rebuilding, as in the case of one that is nearly fifty years old.

The shop utilizes a production line of modest proportions. The white oak ribs are first steamed and then bent over the ancient mold, fitted to the oak keel and stem. All the planks are cut to fit from patterns, and Leo knows each one so well he could probably cut them all by eye. The planks are fastened to the ribs and to the oak transom with bronze screws, then the shell is moved back to the next station for caulking and priming. The boat is turned over, the centerboard case bedded and fastened, and the interior put in place. Cedar flooring serves as the wide cockpit seating, allowing plenty of room to sprawl out in. The deck is added, a

canvas covering put on, and the handsome oak coaming and rails fitted. The spars and rudders are assembled in another part of the shop, where the boats are carefully painted and the trim varnished.

Leo has been a guardian of quality and a teacher and friend of the many who have worked in the shop over the years, but he is equally well known to those who have bought boats from him — first for themselves and later, perhaps, for their grandchildren. Beetle cats have been shipped all over the country, and one even went to Scorpio, Greece, for young John Kennedy, Jr. Others have turned up in Hawaii, the Bahamas, and the Virgin Islands. In Massachusetts, at West Falmouth Harbor, the Hog Island Racers will often start a field of nearly forty of these boats on a Sunday morning. Leo frequently is seen there and at other local meets, greeting his friends and inspecting his "children."

*   *   *

In the 1960s Florida boatbuilder and designer Clark Mills was asked to come up with

Facing page: Leo Telesmanick has supervised the building of thousands of Beetle cats, most of which have been planked up on the same mold, used since 1960.

Built by the thousands in garages and basements, the Optimist Pram is an inexpensive way to learn to sail, and despite its small size (10 feet), it's a lively sailer.

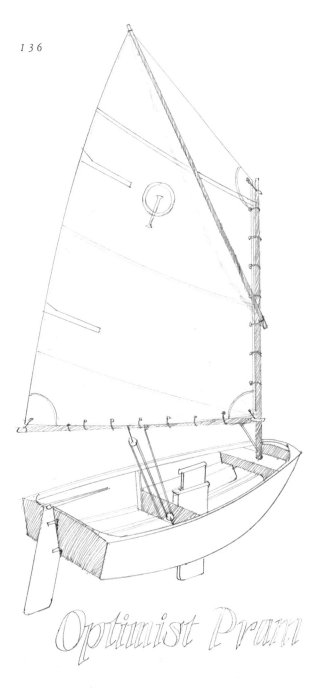

Optimist Pram

a boat that could be home-built, perhaps by a parent and child combination, and used for sail training and club racing. The result was the Optimist Pram — a simple, sprit-rigged daggerboard boat that is safe for children but lively enough for spirited competition. Thousands of these have now been built.

This was part of the plan and kit boom, when many a first boat came out of the pages of *Popular Mechanics*. Relying mostly on lumberyard materials, many clever designs were available, sometimes adapted from traditional dories, skiffs, canoes, and motorboats. Accompanied by step-by-step building manuals, these were suitable for low-cost construction at home. For those less sure of their naval architecture, kits provided precut panels and parts, making the job both easier and faster. A recent survey by *Small Boat Journal* indicates several hundred plans currently on the market, with a substantial number available as kits.

Philip Bolger of Gloucester, Massachusetts, is designer and developer of a large number of plans for simply built, if sometimes unorthodox, small craft. Dynamite Payson of South Thomaston, Maine, has built and marketed plans for some of Bolger's designs and believes anyone can build a boat. Payson has devised a means of construction that seems as far removed from plank-on-frame as one can get. Basically, plywood parts are either cut out from patterns or lofted from plans and then "sewn" together by twisting short wires along the joining edges through small holes. Fiberglass is then applied inside and out. With modern epoxies, this makes a strong joint and does not require frames or molds. Step-by-step photographs show the procedure, and voilà — instant boat! The resultant craft may not be suitable for crossing oceans, but if carefully built, it is a sound recreational vessel.

Harold "Dynamite" Payson at work on a plywood rowing boat.

CHAPTER NINE

THE
TRADITION
CONTINUES

In 1975 a young Maine boatbuilder named Jon Wilson decided to start a newsletter for wooden-boat builders. At that time there was a revival of interest in wooden boats, but it was not receiving much attention from the press. Being independent, as boatbuilders tend to be, Jon started his publication in a remote area of midcoast Maine in a cabin, with the telephone nailed to a tree outside. Today, *WoodenBoat* is published from a handsome brick mansion, though still in the outback in Brooklin, Maine. With a circulation of 100,000, it is a phenomenal success story in the annals of specialty magazine publishing. Its pages not only reflect the glories of past boats and builders, but also focus on the many shops today that build both fine re-creations and innovative contemporary designs.

This and other publications have helped keep their readers informed of our maritime heritage. In addition, there are an expanding number of small boat shops, and thus small craft continue to be a part of contemporary life. The variations are growing too, with powerboats, fishing boats, white-water boats, catamarans, windsurfers, almost any means you can possibly imagine to get on the water. There is even a little high-tech pedal-powered craft called the Waterbug, a sort of egg-shaped ballasted device to scoot in and around the harbor. And the automobile industry tried to get into the act when in the 1970s it introduced the Amphicar, which was advertised as being capable of being driven off the highway and into the lake. Some silly, some clever, and many elegant small watercraft are available to us, most owing a great deal to the traditional working craft described in this book.

Plastics and mass production have made even more boats accessible to an ever-growing public interested in both modern and traditional types. Many of the classic watercraft have been faithfully reproduced in fiberglass and are reasonably priced. Some people, however, opt for wooden versions, and though this market is much smaller, there are a substantial number of shops offering quality custom boatbuilding.

The Dory

Among the first small boats to make it to our shores was the dory. Although its pedigree is uncertain, the dory has been in evidence for a long time. An early Albrecht Dürer watercolor done in 1497 shows a boat that looks remarkably like an eighteenth-century dory. Recorded history tends to show the modern dory being used by the French and Portuguese in the salt-cod trade on the Grand Banks off Newfoundland. Originally, cod fishing was done from the sides of the ship, but when trawl fishing evolved, the ships carried eight or ten small dories to be lowered over the sides. While simple in design, dories are among the most

seaworthy small boats ever devised. Initially quite tender due to their narrow bottom, when loaded with fish they could ride out all but the most violent storms at sea and were capable of carrying large amounts of gear. It takes some skill to handle a dory, but these fishermen were experts.

The simplicity of the dory's construction, combined with its seaworthiness, made it the first "kit" boat. Since dories often went astray from the mother ship, were destroyed, or fell apart, they needed to be replaced frequently, but this was not a simple matter. Early on there were no builders alongshore, nor was there any room on board to carry extra boats. The ship could accommodate several of these boats dissembled and stacked up in the hold, however, ready to be nailed together on any beach. With the development of the American fishing schooner, the dory became an important part of the trade.

The oldest boat shop in America still in operation is Lowell's, in Amesbury, Massachusetts. Here, up until the end of the dory-fishing trade around 1940, thousands of Grand Banks dories were turned out, for not only was the fishing fleet large, but dories were

Facing page: In the winter of 1883, Howard Blackburn, a Gloucester fisherman, went astray in his dory in a dense fog, and miraculously survived a 65-mile, five-day row back to the Newfoundland coast. During that time he let his hands freeze around the oars so he would be able to control the boat. The feat is testament both to the courage of the Grand Banks fishermen and to the seaworthiness of the dory.

expendable boats and generally needed replacing at least once a season. Because of the demand, these boats had to be built quickly, cheaply, and efficiently. In the record year of 1911 the shop turned out more than two thousand dories, or nearly forty a week. A contemporary account of the personnel in the shop at that time follows:

> 4 men sawing and milling boards
> 1 man sharpening tools
> 2 men making bottoms (called "skillets")
> 2 men planking and finishing on 2 beds (forms)
> 2 men general labor
> 2 men painting
> 1 man making frames
> 1 man making stems
> 1 man making transoms and rail caps

Modern efficiency experts would be impressed with these sixteen men, especially since none of them had the luxury of picking up an electric Skilsaw, walking over to an electric drill press, or using a paint gun to speed up the job. A dory doesn't have many pieces — three bottom planks, six side planks, a stem, a transom, some cleats, five frames, four seats, and some trim — and each man knew his job

well, but their production is remarkable by modern standards just the same.

The exploded view of the parts of the dory illustrates how the components could be carried aboard ship to be assembled onshore if the need arose. The planking was always of northern white pine, which is soft and shock absorbent as well as lightweight and fairly rot resistant.

Eventually, the Banks dory trade fell off. The fishing fleets had begun to trawl with nets and carried only two dories on deck for lifesaving purposes, so the dories did not have to be replaced as often. The round-sided surf dory, however, proved its worth to the Life Saving Service (later called the Coast Guard), especially at Newburyport, Massachusetts, though many Lowell boats were shipped across the country. North Pole explorer Donald MacMillan even reported seeing one drawn by an Eskimo on an arctic ice floe.

During World War II Lowell's produced thousands of dories for the armed forces. Ralph Lowell believed in the future of his shop and added a showroom, painting the buildings white instead of the traditional dory brown. By this time Lowell's had built approximately 250,000

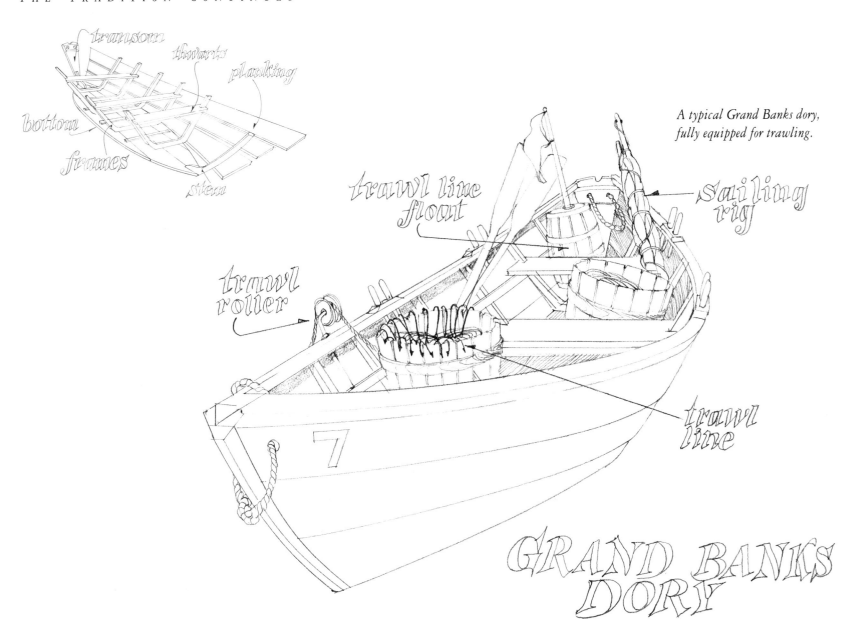

transom

thwarts

planking

bottom

frames

stem

A typical Grand Banks dory,
fully equipped for trawling.

trawl line
float

sailing
rig

trawl
roller

trawl
line

7

GRAND BANKS
DORY

The Lowell Boat Shop, on the banks of the Merrimack River in Amesbury, Massachusetts, is the oldest boat shop in America still in operation.

dories. One indication of the company's long history is the floor on the lower level of the original shop. Although it appears to be merely flecked with paint, the floor is actually covered with more than 7 inches of the stuff. Since the dories were workboats, the objective was to get a thick coat of paint on them, well soaked in, and never mind the yacht finish. The workers would mix up a bucket of paint made of turpentine, white lead, oil, and some ochre powder — enough to do the inside of one boat — dump the pail of paint in the dory bottom, spreading it about until everything was coated, then turn the boat over to do the outside. Thus gradually appeared the built-up floor, and a permanent reminder of a long history.

Since the seaworthiness of the Lowell dory was proven, the company continuously modified it to suit new uses. With the advent of the outboard engine, a well and a broader transom made it a good commercial fishing skiff. A smaller version was built for rowing liveries, and this dory skiff became the official boat supplied to Boy Scout camps across the country. A large 25-foot ocean skiff was developed to use a Palmer inboard motor.

*In spite of its size, this large
dory is surprisingly easy to row.*

Nevertheless, the number of commercial boat shops dwindled by the late 1950s, and though Lowell's still had a reputation for good boats, orders were few and qualified builders even fewer. Fortunately, Fred Tarbox came to work at Lowell's in 1959. Fred is a man with extraordinary skill and the ability to inspire and teach younger builders the art. When the last of the Lowell family decided to sell the shop, Jim Odell bought it on the condition that Fred remain. Thus, the history of the shop has

continued unbroken, though most of the market today is for recreational craft.

Reflecting today's needs, the shop turns out between thirty and sixty boats a year, from 7-foot prams to 24-foot ocean skiffs. Some are equipped with outboard or inboard motors, some with sails, and some with both. The smaller boats are exceptionally easy to row, as they have always been, and when interest in rowing as recreation began to appear, Fred Tarbox recalled Lowell's "fine old rowing boat" and expressed the opinion that people might again enjoy rowing it. After a little research, Fred Tarbox and Jim Odell re-created the boat that had been known during the Civil War as a "gentleman's rowing skiff," and the Salisbury Point rowing skiff is today one of the shop's most popular products. Further reflecting the times, a slimmer, lighter version of this skiff has been added, with a sliding outrigger device for the exercise fan.

The Lowell dory skiff is a handsome and enduring design. It seems to be capable of being scaled up or down in size without losing either its grace or its seaworthiness. In its smallest form it makes a fine yacht tender or child's rowboat. The 15-footer is lively under sail, and the 24-foot ocean skiff is a strong workboat under power or a very able cruiser under sail. All are beachable, and with the addition of epoxy glues and finishes for the bottom, combined with a modern penetration oil topsides finish, the boats require minimal maintenance.

The Whitehall

A boat that had its beginnings in salt water is today finding increased popularity on the lakes and rivers of America as well. The Whitehall pulling boat originated about 1820 as a runner's boat around the New York waterfront, taking its name from nearby Whitehall Street. As large sailing vessels approached the harbor, their crews were met by runners who came aboard huckstering for local brothels, ship chandlers, and the like, eager to separate the poor sailors from their money.

A similar boat now being built by Shew and Burnham is a version of the Whitehall used in Boston, which was not only used for meeting ships, but also rowed competitively by the local clubs. The modern Whitehall is a 12-footer, which serves both as a yacht tender and as a good recreational sailboat.

Dick Shew and Cecil Burnham started building traditional lapstraked small boats full-time in 1968 and have sold more than one hundred fifty to an ever-appreciative clientele. The boats are planked with northern white cedar, have black locust stems, keels, sternposts, and transoms, and will stand very hard use. Dick is former manager of Fuller's yard in East Boothbay, Maine, where he supervised the

This 12-foot *Whitehall built by
Shew and Burnham has
planking made of northern white
cedar, and stem, keel, and
framing of black locust.*

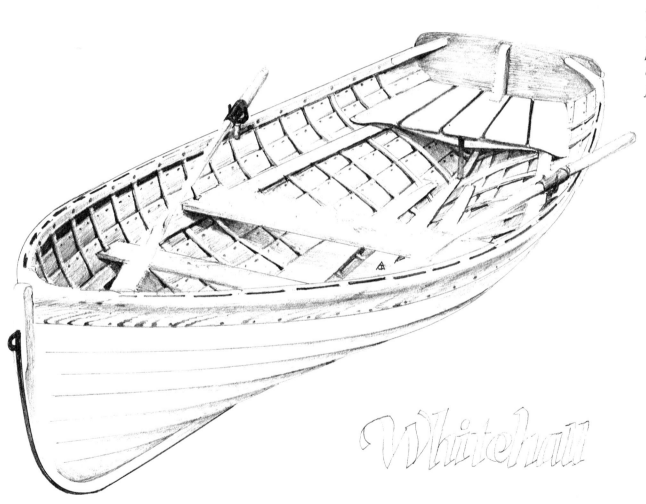

Dick Shew and Cecil Burnham
work on a Whitehall in their
shop in South Bristol, Maine.

building of draggers for the New England fishing fleet. He met Cecil later while working in another yard where Cecil was lofting wooden powerboats. When shipbuilding in wood began to decline, Dick built a few Whitehalls on the side, and as they caught on, he decided to open his own shop.

The shop, a nice place to be, rambles through two stories. Downstairs is for the heavy machinery — an old but accurate assortment of planers, bandsaws, shapers, and other exotic-looking special tools — while upstairs is where the boats take shape on old molds that have seen countless craft coaxed into shape with sharp, well-cared-for hand tools. The shop is cluttered, and a lot of shavings and odds and ends are scattered about, but there is a sense of purpose and pride here. The shop spills out onto the property — molds for different sizes, old boats turned upside down on sawhorses, new boats awaiting shipment.

What one sees in the workshop is a simple, uncomplicated approach to a highly skilled trade. The men's attitude is not unlike the work ethic prevalent in most shops a hundred years ago, though the production is tempered by

modern methods and business practices
necessary to be competitive in the current
market.

The Hampton

Another fine example of a contemporary
use and interpretation of a traditional watercraft
is Richard Pulsifer's Hampton boat. Dick has a
shop on Casco Bay, Maine, where he has built
more than two dozen of these strip-planked
powerboats, based on an earlier Hampton
design by Charles Gomes. (The history of this
boat is found in Chapter Four.) What is
significant is that Pulsifer has managed to refine,
but not change, a one-hundred-year-old
building method and turn out a highly efficient
modern powerboat.

The Hampton uses a 15- to 22-
horsepower diesel engine of contemporary design
— replacing the heavier traditional unit with just
the right power-to-weight ratio. I have had the
pleasure of using a Pulsifer Hampton and was
impressed with its smooth ride, sure tracking,
relative quiet, and modest fuel consumption.
This contrasts sharply with a similar "market-

*The Pulsifer Hampton is a fine
example of the many classic
boats being built today — using
modern fastenings and methods
while remaining faithful to the
spirit and function of time-
proven watercraft.*

The Apprenticeshop of the Maine Maritime Museum in Bath, Maine, is situated on the museum's grounds, in the restored Percy and Small Shipyard, which built many of Maine's coastal schooners from 1896 to 1920.

oriented" power cruiser of roughly the same length requiring a big 150-horsepower gas engine to run it as it churns through choppy waters. There is no room aboard a Hampton for a microwave oven or shower, but those conveniences pale in comparison with the pleasures of quiet, leisurely cruising in this well-adapted traditional small boat.

*   *   *

There are many boatbuilding shops around today, each with only one, two, or three builders. The demand for wooden boats is not great enough to justify larger operations, with the exception of the production of established boats such as the Beetle cat and the Lowell skiffs. If the wooden boat had remained popular in the past half century, there would have been an unbroken tradition of apprentice training, but except in rare cases, most of the master builders from the workboat era are gone or retired. Some of the older skills have been in danger of extinction, since boatbuilders are seldom writers and boatbuilding has always required a hands-on rather than a formal verbal education.

Fortunately, with renewed interest in small boats over the past twenty years, boatbuilding schools have begun to appear in various locations, some as outgrowths of museum education programs and others independently conceived to provide vocational training in a much changed but still viable profession. Where possible, these apprentice shops have employed older experienced builders or relied on practiced craftsmen who have acquired the traditional skills. This education fulfills two needs: It keeps alive the knowledge and skills of traditional boatbuilding and design, and it offers a sound learning experience for those who have the desire to adopt this particular way of life.

But the new schools must teach more than spiling, joining, and spar making, for economic competition is fierce. Although traditional boats are gaining in popularity, they must be competitively priced — no small task when you compare hand labor to mass production. There is also a public perception that wooden boats are nice but require a lot of upkeep and won't last as long as fiberglass ones. The four decades that fiberglass has been in use have proved this not to be so: It too ages and has its own special maintenance concerns. Oddly enough, it is the very science of plastics that has given wood a renewed life as a boatbuilding material. Since wood's natural enemy is rot, which cannot occur if water cannot get to the wood, the use of high-grade epoxies as sealants and fastening resins has proved invaluable.

Modern boatbuilders are learning to be good businessmen as well as able builders. In addition to the leading small boat publications, several organizations promote both boatbuilding and boat use. The Traditional Small Craft Association (TSCA), for example, based in Mystic, Connecticut, is very active in holding meets and shows and publishes a fine newsletter. The TSCA was formed to lobby against Coast Guard regulations that threatened to make it difficult for small boats to be legally on the water. In an effort to promote boating safety, the Coast Guard began to require so much safety equipment and such high standards that small boats had a hard time complying. It was largely the notion that bigger is better that led many to think that small boats were unsafe. (How a doryman of 1880 would laugh at that idea.) The TSCA went to work and happily proved the

already two-hundred-year-old fact that most small craft are as safe, if not safer, than some of the newer, bigger boats.

Much of the emphasis in this book has been on wooden boats for the simple reason that wood was the most readily available material during their development. To re-create boats today exactly as they were built in the nineteenth century is a viable notion and provides a satisfying link to our past. But the reason boats were built in the first place was to get on the water, and consequently any material that can successfully accomplish that job is valid. None would agree more with that idea than builders of the past, for they were always trying to improve on technique, materials, and designs.

Today's new materials have the advantage of making boats of all kinds available to a wider market. Some are re-creations of traditional types, and others are innovative modern creations that take advantage of these new materials. But whatever the style and materials, the building goes on, and the tradition of small boats continues.

*   *   *

It is a cool summer morning with a promise of wind and bright sunshine. Though the coast of Maine tends to be foggy in August, today will be clear. I have a lunch packed and a rare opportunity to break off from the day's routine.

As my little sharpie drifts easily down river to the sea on the morning tide, I watch the firs slipping by, cormorants on the rocks drying their wings, and an osprey circling above me. Port Clyde gives way to small islands — perhaps one will be a landing spot for lunch, or I might just drop sail and drift — there's no schedule today.

By afternoon the wind has shifted to the southwest, as it usually does; the air is brisk. As my sharpie boils along steadily with a gentle rise-and-fall rhythm, much of what was so urgent, so important ashore grows a bit hazy, at least for a while. . . .

The late afternoon wind brings me home on an incoming tide. Drifting ashore, I have time to admire the river, the trees, this small boat which seems such a natural part of its surroundings. Although the day has been perfect, there have been others not so easy, with foul tides, sudden squalls, and deep fog. But the boat is a constant, no matter what the weather. It not only sharpens my sense of the world around me, but also enhances my appreciation of those who have built and worked small boats. And I realize that as an artist and writer, I have no edge on their deep love and respect for being on the water.

MARITIME MUSEUMS AND COLLECTIONS

The current interest in small boats has encouraged many of the maritime museums in this country to expand their collections and displays. The emphasis is now on an active rather than a static use of artifacts. Some museums have restored boats or replicas available for demonstrations on the water; others accommodate building and apprenticeship programs, both to teach and preserve skills and to provide the public with an opportunity to observe boatbuilding firsthand.

A number of fine museums reflect our maritime heritage, and the list that follows focuses on those that devote substantial space to small craft.

The Adirondack Museum, Blue Mountain Lake, NY 12812; (518) 352-7311. Primary museum of the Adirondack guide boat; includes canoes and other early small watercraft; regional history and artifacts.

Chesapeake Bay Maritime Museum, St. Michaels, MD 21663; (301) 745-2916. A full collection of the working watercraft of the bay, including skipjacks, tongers, bugeyes, and log canoes. Also includes a waterfowling exhibit.

Herreshoff Marine Museum, Bristol, RI 02890; (401) 253-5000. Operated by Hallsey Herreshoff and located in a building that was once part of the Herreshoff Manufacturing Company, builder of some of the most famous yachts in America; contains the first boat N.G. Herreshoff ever built, various small sailboats and dinghies, and early photographs of half models.

Maine Maritime Museum, Bath, ME 04530; (207) 443-1316. Located on the site of a major shipbuilding facility. Includes a comprehensive permanent exhibit on the lobstering industry, with examples of each type of boat and its development. Also has an apprenticeship program for building traditional small craft.

The Mariners' Museum, Newport News, VA 23606; (804) 595-0368. Extensive model collection, photographs, and archives.

Mystic Seaport Museum, Inc., Mystic, CT 06355; (203) 572-0711. Open year-round. More than forty restored buildings representing a coastal community in the age of sail. Extensive small craft collection.

Peabody Museum of Salem, Salem, MA 01970; (617) 745-1876. Large model collection, exhibits of nautical instruments and boatbuilders' tools, small boat displays.

Penobscot Marine Museum, Searsport, ME 04974; (207) 548-2529. Small craft exhibit, models, and photographs.

Shelburne Museum, Inc., Shelburne, VT 05482; (802) 985-3344. Nautical items, paintings, prints, and canoe exhibit.

South Street Seaport Museum, New York, NY 10038; (212) 669-9400. Displays of New York's maritime history. Boat shop shows building in progress.

Suffolk Marine Museum, West Sayville, NY 11796; (516) 567-1733. Early oyster vessels; history of the Long Island oyster industry.

Thousand Islands Museum, Old Town Hall, Clayton, NY 13624; (315) 686-5794. St. Lawrence River skiff history.

Thousand Islands Shipyard Museum, Clayton, NY 13624; (315) 686-4104. Antique power craft; large collection of small boats.

The Whaling Museum, New Bedford, MA 02740; (617) 997-0046. Whaleships and whaleboats display; fine collections of scrimshaw, marine carvings, paintings, and whaling tools.

RECOMMENDED READING

BOOKS

Bishop, Nathaniel Holmes. *Four Months in a Sneak Box:
A Boat Voyage of Twenty Six Hundred Miles
Down the Ohio & Mississippi Rivers*. Detroit:
Gale Research Co., 1976 (reprint).

Bray, Maynard. *Mystic Seaport Museum Watercraft*.
Mystic, CT: Mystic Seaport Museum, Inc., 1979.

Bruette, William. *American Duck, Goose, and Brant
Shooting*. New York: Charles Scribner's, 1947.

Chapelle, Howard. *American Small Sailing Craft*. New
York: W.W. Norton & Co., Inc., 1951.

Davis, Charles G. *American Sailing Ships*. New York:
Dover Publications, Inc., 1984.

Desmond, Charles. *Wooden Ship-Building*. 2d ed.
(facsimile ed.; orig. 1919). Vestal, NY: Vestal
Press, Ltd., 1984.

Duncan, Roger F. *Friendship Sloops*. Camden, ME:
International Marine Publishing Co., 1985.

Gardner, John. *Building Classic Small Craft*. Camden,
ME: International Marine Publishing Co., 1977.

Gardner, John. *The Dory Book*. Camden, ME:
International Marine Publishing Co., 1979.

Griffin, Carl, III, and Aleric Faulkner. *Coming of Age on
Damariscove Island*. Orono, ME: Northeast
Folklore Society, 1981.

Leavens, John M., ed. *The Catboat Book*. Camden, ME:
International Marine Publishing Co., 1973.

Martin, Kenneth R., and Nathan R. Lipfert. *Lobstering &
the Maine Coast*. Bath, ME: Maine Maritime
Museum, 1985.

New England Beetle Cat Association Handbook. South
Dartmouth, MA: Concordia Company, 1979.

Roberts, Kenneth G., and Philip Shackleton. *The Canoe:
A History of the Craft from Panama to the Arctic*.
Camden, ME: International Marine Publishing
Co., 1983.

Thomas, Gordon W. *Fast & Able, Life Stories of Great
Gloucester Fishing Schooners*. New ed. Paul B.

Kenyon, ed. Rockport, MA: Nelson B.
Robinson, Bookseller, 1973.

Wood, Pamela, ed. *The Salt Book*. New York: Anchor
Press, 1977.

PERIODICALS

Ash Breeze, Traditional Small Craft Association, P.O.
Box 350, Mystic, CT 06355; (203) 536-6342.
A quarterly newsletter containing articles on
traditional boats either being built or
documented. Also contains letters from regional
members and clubs, information on local TSCA
groups.

Messing About In Boats, 29 Burley, Wenham, MA
01984; (617) 774-0906. A comprehensive
publication that is issued biweekly. Features
extensive coverage of small boating events in the
New England area; on-the-spot reporting of
many races, meets, and new boat launchings;
reprints of rare stories from the early 1900s;
articles on many owner-built projects.

Sailing magazine, 125 E. Main Street, Port Washington,
WI 53074; (414) 284-3494. Catering to the
great interest in sailing in the Midwest and Great
Lakes area, this large-format monthly is heavily
pictorial and covers a wide range of subjects,
from small boats to major racing to classic yachts.

Small Boat Journal, Box 1066, Bennington, VT
05201; (802) 442-3101. Dedicated to boats
under 30 feet, this bimonthly covers small
watercraft of all materials and manufacture:
wood, fiberglass, and aluminum. Boat reviews,
sailing trials, product directories, and special
issues such as kayaking, boatbuilding, etc.
are featured.

WoodenBoat, Box 78, Brooklin, ME 04616; (207) 359-
4651. A bimonthly dedicated to the preservation,
documentation, and continuing evolution of
wooden boats. Step-by-step articles on small
boats; in-depth historical retrospectives on classic
yachts, designers, and builders; technical articles
on materials and methods; reports on new
designs.

INDEX